TRAVIS FORD:
BIG BLUE DREAM

To Judy + Judy!
Go Big - Blue!

Travis Ford
5

TRAVIS

FORD

BIG BLUE DREAM

Travis Ford

and

Tom Wallace

Butler Books
Louisville, Kentucky

For my coaches and teammates, who made
it so much fun; and most especially, for my parents,
my sister and Kim, who stood by me all the way
and helped me make my dream come true.
— *T.F.*

For my mother, my sister and the memory
of my father; and for Joe Boggs, friend,
mentor and landlord extraordinaire.
— *T.W.*

CONTENTS

FOREWORD

I'm sitting here trying to decide what to say about Travis Ford, and I realize that there isn't much that hasn't already been said about him and his basketball career. Everyone is familiar with Travis's story: a great high school career at Madisonville North Hopkins; a recruiting dilemma his senior year of high school; a great freshman season at Missouri; a transfer to Kentucky; an injury-plagued sophomore year; an outstanding junior season; and a solid senior campaign. That's what you see when you look at it from the outside. However, a closer look shows us an individual who through hard work and with a big heart has managed to overcome many obstacles. Whether it was doubts due to his lack of size, or a coach who thought Travis's motives were too selfish, Travis managed to define the situation and make the needed adjustments. Every young basketball player can learn something from Travis, and it's not just how to shoot free throws. "T Ford" is living proof of the old adage that "if you want to do something bad enough, and are willing to pay the price, you can be successful."

Basketball has always been a family thing for Travis. While many people know Travis's father, Eddie, and always see him involved in the game, few know that it is his mother, Pat, who is the steadying force behind the scene. Both are proud parents and No.1 fans who have spent countless hours following their son and watching his basketball career unfold.

Being the color analyst for the University of Kentucky Radio Network allows me some privileges. I am able to watch practices daily and get to know the players much better than the average fan does. Having played at UK, I also understand many things the players go through, both on and off the court.

Sure, Travis' senior year may not have lived up to everyone else's expectations, and we all know that it ended sooner than he would have liked. But the thing that impressed me most was how Travis handled his last year as a Wildcat. First of all, to make 50 free throws in a row is phenomenal. That record will stand for a long time. Then, with the talent pool considerably less proven than the year before, Travis instantly became a marked man. Opposing teams figured that if they could stop Travis, they could stop Kentucky. Most players who were constantly being double-teamed would have started forcing shots out of frustration. Not Travis. Instead, he concentrated on getting more assists, sometimes to the point that he turned down good shots. Yes, the same guy I used to watch during his redshirt year trying to beat five pressing defenders by dribbling full-court now understood that by distributing the ball, he would make his teammates better.

As time passes, fans remember the players for one particular game or one particular play. For me, I won't remember Travis for the 50 free throws, or the 29 points against Indiana, or even the fade-away three-pointer from deep in the corner against Florida to give Kentucky the lead after a 19-point deficit. Instead, I'll remember Travis most for something he did before he even went to college. It showed me what he was made of.

Back then, when Travis was coming out of high school, the University of Kentucky was hosting a national AAU tournament. Players from all over the country were on campus. Coaches from all over were here to scout the players. During one session, I happened to be sitting next to Bobby Cremins, the head coach at Georgia Tech. At the time, Bobby was looking for a point guard. He told me he was not convinced that Travis could play major college basketball. Then Bobby asked me my opinion. About that time, Travis got cold-cocked by a blind pick, but instead of coming off the court, he picked himself up and instantly went down the floor and scored three baskets in a row. I don't know what Bobby Cremins thought, but that play made me a believer.

Travis never used his lack of size, or any other deficiencies, as an excuse. Rather, he used them as a motivational tool. Coaches can teach fundamentals and skills, but they can't teach a player to have heart. And when it is all said and done, having heart may have been Travis's biggest asset. People ask me if he can make it in the NBA. I don't know. But I do know that it isn't wise to tell Travis that he can't do something. If you do, you'd better be prepared for a fight. So, I would not bet against him.

The University of Kentucky has always produced great backcourt players. Ralph Beard, Kenny Rollins, Vernon Hatton and Louie Dampier, just to name a few. As the years keep rolling by, and as that UK tradition continues, Travis Ford will always know that he belongs on that list.

— *Kyle Macy , Lexington, Ky. March 31, 1994*

INTRODUCTION

At the Southeastern Conference basketball tournament in Memphis, a sports writer, after finishing an interview with Travis Ford said, "You know, Travis, your story is an interesting one. You should think about doing a book." That insightful scribe couldn't possibly have known at the time that his suggestion would soon become reality.

Travis Ford does have a story to tell. It is a story that touches us in different ways. It is all about dreaming big dreams, and having the courage and fortitude to make them come true. It is about having to constantly prove the doubters wrong. It is about going from the backyard to the pinnacle of college basketball, from playing imaginary games alone to performing in front of thousands of spectators. It is about making mistakes and learning from them. It is about following in footsteps, then leaving your own for others to follow. It is about overcoming big odds. Most of all, though, Travis's story is about family, both on and off the court.

In some ways, his is an old-fashioned story, and perhaps that's one of the reasons why it strikes a chord in all of us. We live in a fast-paced, high-tech world that chews up and spits out its values like they were watermelon seeds, yet here's a guy who genuinely loves his family, appreciates his teammates, and respects his coaches. Plus, he happens to be a nice person. It's almost too good to be true.

Being the writer who was fortunate enough to put Travis's words and thoughts on the printed page has provided me with the opportunity to get to know Travis in a very real way. I was not unfamiliar with Travis when we began this project. I covered the Wildcats for seven years as the editor of "Cawood on Kentucky". However I was most familiar with him as a basketball player. That is the way most people know him. Writing this book has allowed me to see a different side of him.

Unless you are around the UK basketball players, and in particular, one as popular as Travis, you cannot begin to appreciate what they go through. The demands made of them are enormous. How would you like it if you could not go to a movie, or go out to eat with your family, or just walk in a mall without being asked to sign a hundred autographs or have your picture taken a dozen times? There's a tradeoff for UK players — the loss of privacy for the right to wear the blue and white. It has always been that way, and it always will be that way.

I have been around Travis for four years now and I cannot remember ever once seeing him behave in an arrogant, curt, or unpleasant way when he has been approached by fans seeking autographs, pictures, a handshake, or just a simple hello. He has always conducted himself in an honest, kind and generous way, even when time constraints or circumstances prevented him from fulfilling the fans' wishes. Travis Ford has been, in every way, a class act, a credit to his family, and a credit to the University of Kentucky.

After talking with Travis, it's clear to me that he cares more about his teammates than himself. Time after time, Travis praises them for what they have meant to his basketball career and to him as a person. That is one of the threads that runs though his story. And it is not false or insincere praise, either. He means it. Travis is wise enough to know that the journey to the top can't be completed without a lot of assistance along the way. It's just rare these days to find an athlete so willing to acknowledge it.

Speaking of assistance, there are several people I want to thank for helping me complete this project. Without them, I couldn't have written this book. Thanks to Pat and Eddie Ford for their help and letting me sift through the family archives. Their generosity contributed greatly to the final product. My thanks to good friend Jim Pickens for double-checking the facts, particularly those concerning Travis's high school career. Jim was the sports editor for the Madisonville Messenger at the time, and the person who chronicled Travis's prep exploits in detail. Thanks to publisher Bill Butler for his confidence and his expert advice. A very special thanks to Marilyn Underwood for the difficult task of putting the spoken word onto paper. Her effort was tremendous. And, finally, the biggest thanks of all to Travis for being so patient with me and so open about his life, and for fighting through the discomfort of talking about himself. Thanks for sharing your story with us.

—T.W.

I. DREAMING BIG

CHAPTER ONE

BITTERSWEET ENDING

Mixed emotions, that's probably the best way I can explain my feelings as I looked up at the scoreboard and watched the final seconds ticking away, knowing that we weren't going to pull off one last miracle comeback, knowing that we weren't going to escape the grave one final time. Our season, which had been marked by an endless series of adversities, a season of ups and downs, was officially over. Marquette had upset us in the second round of the NCAA Tournament, ending our dream of returning to the Final Four for a second straight year. There would be no NCAA championship in 1993-94 for the Kentucky Wildcats. Sitting on the bench, having fouled out late in the game, I looked at my jersey and realized that it was the last time I would ever wear it. My college career had come to an end. That was a tough moment for me. Never again would I put on a Kentucky Wildcat uniform, a uniform I had been both proud and privileged to wear for the past three years. Never again would I be with my teammates and coaches, wonderful people who had gone through so much together in an effort to achieve excellence.

Never again would I perform in front of all those great Big Blue fans who had supported us through good times and bad times. Like I said, it was a tough, emotional moment. On the one hand, I was proud of what this team had accomplished, of what I had accomplished.

On the other hand, I was disappointed because of the way we had played against Marquette, of the way I had played. Every player on the team truly believed that we could get to the Final Four and win it all. Now it was over, and I think we all felt that we had let ourselves and the fans down. As I walked off the court for the final time, Coach Pitino came up to me, gave me a hug, and whispered in my ear, "It's been great." Hearing that from him, a man I respect so much, a man who helped me develop into a better person and a better basketball player, meant everything to me. In the locker room, it really hit me that my career had come to an end. The thing I felt most was how fast it had gone by. It seemed like only yesterday that I was two or three years old and going to watch my father's teams play. Suddenly, the time span between my first Junior Pro games and my last game as a Kentucky Wildcat didn't seem that wide. Strangely, though, every game and every memory is as clear to me today as it was when it happened, and each one will be treasured forever.

Looking back, I understand how fortunate I've been. Few people are as lucky, or as blessed. Believe me, it's not something I take lightly. Because of the support I've had from family, friends, coaches and teammates, I've been able to live my dream. It's been a marvelous experience, and a wonderful trip that has taken me from the smallest gyms in Hopkins County to the largest arenas around the country. I have played with and against some of the greatest basketball players of all time. I've been coached by several of the finest coaches to ever diagram a play on a chalkboard. And I've done it all in front of thousands of fans who understand and appreciate good basketball.

Who could have asked for more?

There is no way I can begin to adequately thank everyone who has helped me along the way. No athlete can see his dream come true without the support of countless people, many of whom help without even realizing it. That's certainly true in my case. My father, Don Parson, Coach Pitino, Norm Stewart: they are the obvious influences. Everyone knows about them and what they've meant in my life. But behind the scenes there have been hundreds of people who have encouraged me, taught me, and supported me in ways that made my basketball career possible. To each and every one of them, I offer my eternal gratitude. I wouldn't be where I am today without their help. If my story has a message, if my achievements have any meaning at all, I would hope that it's as an inspiration to the "little guys" with the big dreams. You can make those dreams come true if you're willing to pay the price. It's not easy, especially in a sport like basketball, and you're always going to hear people tell you it can't be done. Don't listen. Those people don't know what they're talking about. It *can* be done. Just hang in there and never give up. You can make your dreams come true. I'm proof that it can happen.

CHAPTER TWO

BEGINNINGS

My love for basketball must be in the genes. That's the only way I can figure it, the only reasonable explanation I can come up with. Nothing else makes much sense. I have loved the sport of basketball for as long as I can remember. So long, in fact, that I often feel certain that I was born with a wide-seam Rawlings RSS in my hands.

Given the background of my parents, my passion for basketball is really easy to explain. My father, Eddie, was a superb player at South Hopkins High School and at Murray. He later became a successful high school coach. My mother, Pat, who is originally from Daviess County, also did some coaching. So their influence was always present, even if I wasn't consciously aware of it. I was always fascinated by balls. Any type of ball. I loved having one with me, rolling it, bouncing it, throwing it. I just loved the feel of it. According to my mom, I had my first goal when I was still in the crib. Basketball was there for me right from the beginning.

Having parents who coached was heaven for me. When

I was just two or three years old, I'd go to their practices and just run around the gym with a basketball in my hands. That's really about all I could do. I couldn't dribble at the time, and I was too small and too weak to shoot. But the experience of being in the gym, being around older players, just being in that great atmosphere, all of that had a big influence on me.

Naturally, I'd go to every one of their games. I can still remember most of the players. I was fascinated by the game even then, how fast-paced it was, the running, the shooting, the jumping, all of it. I remember the first time I ever saw a player dunk the ball. He was playing against my father's team. I couldn't believe anyone could do that; it just blew me away.

My father put up my first goal for me at home when I was four or five. It wasn't very high, but there was a reason for that. My father always believed the height of a goal is very important. It shouldn't be so high that I couldn't make the shot. As I got older and stronger, he'd raise it. But, even when I was in the eighth or ninth grade and had a regulation-size goal, I still had a smaller one as well so that I could dunk and do different things. My father's belief is that if the goal is too high, then younger players, in an effort to make the shot, will develop bad habits.

I have always said — and still believe — that my father knows more basketball than anyone I've ever been around. Coach Pitino is the best teacher of basketball I've ever been associated with, but my father is the most knowledgeable. His understanding of the game, of all aspects of the game, is remarkable. I wish he had continued coaching. I'm convinced he would have been a great one.

You have to remember, my father wasn't just some guy talking about something he didn't know. He'd been a player, a three-year starter at South Hopkins and a starter at Murray State. I've had people tell me that he was a great shooter and a smart player on the court. A lot of people say I remind them of him, that I'm a smaller version of him. So he's not some fan just doing a lot of talking. When it comes to basketball, he knows his subject.

I want to stop the myth that my father forced me, relentlessly pushed me into playing basketball.That is absolutely not the case at all. My father never, ever, pushed me to play. If anything, the reverse is true. He probably didn't help me as much as he could have. He was very conscious of that, of not wanting to force me to do something just because he loved it and maybe wanted to see me follow in his footsteps. My mother was by far more aggressive in that respect than he was. Many times, I would be outside playing by myself and she'd get all over dad, telling him that he should be out there playing with me, teaching me. But it was important to my dad that I wanted to play on my own, that the love of the game was inside me. If it was, great; if not, he wasn't going to force me to play.

The love, of course, was there from the beginning. And so was my father. He was always there to help me whenever I had a question. Ball-handling drills were among the first fundamentals that he taught me. Handling the ball came easily to me. I can't explain why, but it did. And the more I handled it, the more things I learned to do, the more fascinated I became. That fascination really started when I first learned to spin a ball on my finger. Then I taught myself how to pitch the ball in the air, catch it on my fingertip and keep it spinning. One trick led to another, until I became extremely good at handling the ball. I had a ball in my hands so much that it became a part of me. I've said all along that even though I don't have very big hands, the reason I can palm a basketball is because it's part of my hand. All of that came about because of my father, but only because I really wanted it and not because he was pushy or dominating.

I can't stress enough my natural love for basket ball. I can't even fully understand it. All I can say is that it's very real, and I've had it for as long as I can remember. Even when I started school, my interest was basketball. I wasn't like the other kids. For instance, when I was in kindergarden, once or twice a week we'd have show and tell. We'd bring in different things and talk about them. Some might bring in a model airplane or the family dog. All kinds of different things. Not me. Every single time, I would bring in my basketball. One time, I would show them how I could spin it on my finger; the next time, I would dribble between my legs. They never knew what I was going to do next, but they could be sure it would be with a basketball.

I went to Hanson Elementary School through the sixth grade. I was lucky because there were several other guys at Hanson who were equally serious about basketball. Guys like Jason Adams and Scotty Martin. While most of the other boys saw recess as a time for recreation, we saw it as time for some serious basketball.

Like most boys our age, we were influenced by older players. My dad would take me to watch Madisonville play and one of my first heroes was Jeff Martin. He was the first player I actually followed. Another influence was Craig Bass. I remember how athletic he was. I used to watch them and dream about the day when I could get out there and play.

But Kyle Macy was my biggest hero. I basically worshiped him at the time. I think I liked him so much because of the way he shot free throws, the way he would wipe his hands on his socks. He was such a great shooter, such a great player. One of my earliest big thrills was when I met him. It was after he'd graduated from UK and had come to Madisonville for a personal appearance.

By this time, my father was out of coaching and in the sporting goods business. He owned a sporting goods store in Madisonville. He also had his own basketball camp. Because of that I had the chance to meet several big-name players. Artis Gilmore came by the store once, and Louie Dampier. It was a great experience for me to be around people who were so good at the game. It couldn't help but have a positive impact on me.

Although I loved Kyle Macy and followed UK, the team I first wanted to play for was Murray. I used to tell everyone that if I could play anywhere in the world, it would be for Murray. That's because my father played there. And Chris Rhodes' father went to Murray. Chris is one of my best friends; he and I always went to Murray games together. We had a great hatred of Western at the time. Murray and Western were huge rivals, so we didn't like Western at all.

My first taste of organized ball came when I started playing junior pro. That was an interesting time. I was playing for my dad, but what I remember most is that my temper got me in a lot of trouble. I had a terrible, terrible temper. Because I was such a competitor at an early age I hated losing, and I hated anybody telling me I was doing something wrong. I'm proud that I had a fierce desire to win but I'm not proud of how I handled myself back then.

Dad has a pretty quick temper, so I guess I got it from him. He doesn't get mad all that often, but when he does, he lets you know. I saw that when he was coaching.

My temper got the best of me more times than I care to admit. When it did, I would get in trouble twice, at the gym because my father was the coach, then again at home when I had to answer to my mom. It was just immaturity and stupidity on my part. I would get terribly upset whenever my father tried to correct me or say something to help me. I would take it personally, convinced that he was chewing me out because I was his son. I would pout, throw basketballs, refuse to talk to him, all kinds of dumb things. I would get so mad that it affected my game. I'd go out and foul somebody on purpose or yell at the referee. I got many technicals at an early age.

Considering how badly I behaved my dad was pretty cool. He never said that much to me, just things like, "Hey, watch it." But my mom was different. She was pretty strict. She always tried to make me understand that my father was only doing it for my benefit. However, if I kept it up, she'd get very angry with me. My mom has pretty much always been on my side and she knew that if I kept getting mad it was only going to hurt me.

The great blessing I've had is strong family support. I had it at the beginning, and it continues to this very day. Unbelievable support. My mother and father were always there for me, during bright days or dark days. So has my sister Leslie and her husband, Tore, my aunt and uncle and my nephew Ford who calls me Choo Choo. They never miss a game; if I played in Alaska, they'd all be there. That kind of backing makes things much easier and much more enjoyable for me.

I played junior pro for three years and during that time I made my first road trip as a player. I was eight or nine. Our all-star team came to Lexington to compete for the state championship. We played at Transylvania College against a team called Mary Todd. We came out on the court to shoot layups, then looked down at the other end and those guys were *dunking*. We were all wondering, "What have we gotten ourselves into?" We hung with them for a long time, but they ended up beating us in the first game.

We got our revenge the next year, beating Mary Todd 28-23 in the first round. Alan Hall and I had nine points each in that game. We beat Scott County 36-26 in the next game, then lost to Campbell County 44-28. Alan and I both made the all-tournament team.

When I was in the fifth grade, I competed in a national free throw shooting contest and won at the local and regional levels. That meant I got to go to Lexington for the state finals. The Kyle Macy influence was paying off. I always enjoyed shooting free throws, probably because I was always good at it. But there's no doubt in my mind that because of Kyle, I took free throws very seriously. I think I concentrated more and understood their importance when I started watching and emulating him.

When we got to Lexington, the final competition was between me and a guy named Earnest "June Bug" Rakes . June Bug would later go on to have a good career at Kentucky Wesleyan. He had won the national championship the year before, so I had heard of him. I was extremely nervous, but I ended up making 22 out of 25 shots. Unfortunately, he made 24 out of 25. That really upset me. I hate losing more than anything in the world.

However learning to deal with losing is something all athletes must do. No one wins all the time, regardless of how good he or she might be. Whenever I lose, or whenever I don't think I've played up to my potential, I become very quiet. I don't like talking about it. I know what I did or didn't do, so the last thing I need is for someone to come up to me and start telling me what they think I did wrong. In the past I think that caused people to misread me. They attribute it to my temper or my attitude, but they're wrong. It isn't that at all. I just prefer to deal with it by myself.

I understand that there's a fundamental difference between playing badly and losing and hitting 22 of 25 free throws and losing. Hitting 22 of 25 is pretty good. But the only thing I see is that I lost. Came in second. Got the smaller trophy. Period. I don't want someone congratulating me for finishing second. The way I see it, I should have made 25 out of 25. Maybe I should have practiced a little bit more, or been stronger mentally.

I don't refuse to give the other guy credit though. "June Bug" won, so I tip my hat to him. I have a whole lot of confidence in myself but I'm smart enough to know if somebody is a little better than I am. Still, I always feel that there is something I can do to compensate, something that will make me better than my opponent. The trick is to find that something.

I've often reflected on where all this confidence comes from. Was I born with it or did I pick it up along the way? After much thought, I've become convinced that it comes from two sources.

First, it came from my mother and father, from the support they gave me. They constantly told me that if I worked hard enough, I could accomplish anything. I heard that so often from them that I began thinking, "Yes, I can do it and if

I don't, then it's my own fault." They instilled in me a great belief in myself. I figured if they had that much faith in me, then I must be pretty good.

Second, I think my confidence was greatly enhanced because I was the son of two coaches. One of the things you always hear is that coaches' sons are fundamentally more sound than most players and that they have a better understanding, a better grasp, of the game. I don't think there's any doubt about that. It's true. That comes from being around the game so much. If you go to games and to practice then you're always in the gym. You pick things up even when you don't realize it. In my case, both parents had been coaches. Sure, I was born with some talent, I won't deny that, but I learned most of what I know from growing up with it. Other guys were on the playground, playing; I was in the gym, learning.

Basketball was my all-consuming passion. I played all the time, year-round. Girls didn't exist for me. I simply never paid any attention to them. If I wasn't in a gym, I was in my backyard, playing alone, pretending to be Kyle Macy. I never lost either. I always took the last shot, the game-winning shot, and if I missed, it was because I was fouled. In that case, I'd win the game with a couple of free throws. I don't guess I was much different from a million other Kentucky boys who dreamed of playing for the Wildcats.

In the real world however, away from the Rupp Arena of my backyard, there were realities to face. The number one reality I constantly dealt with was perception.Namely, other people's perception that I was too small to ever be a successful basketball player. That stigma has trailed me,sometimes even preceded me, for much of my life. It began in grade school and has, in one way or another, stayed with me up until now.

"Too small." "A nice player, but he can't make it at the next level." "No way he can play Division I ball." "If he were only a couple of inches taller, he'd be something special."

There's no way to accurately count the number of times I've heard statements like that. No matter what I did, no matter how well I played, always there were doubters. I sometimes felt the skeptics far outnumbered the believers. That was perfectly fine with me, because I love nothing more than proving the skeptics wrong. It's just another challenge to be met, another hurdle to be cleared.

What they never understood is that I didn't picture myself as being that small. So what if other players were bigger than I was? It never once dawned on me that you had to be big in order to be a good basketball player until people starting telling me that I was good now, but when I got older I wouldn't be as effective. I remember hearing that and just shaking my head. It was absurd.

Those doubters failed to take several important factors into consideration. My heart and my determination, for starters. My desire to be a good basketball player. And my willingness to pay whatever price it takes to overcome big odds. I simply wasn't about to let size keep me from achieving what I knew I had the talent and ability to achieve, regardless of what anyone else's perception might be. To use size as an excuse to fail is a major league cop-out.

Size, for me, wasn't going to be a factor. OK, so I wasn't the tallest guy in the world. So what? I was what I was, so I had to make the best of it. If it meant I had to work harder to succeed, that's what I would do. If it meant more practice, then I'd stay longer in the gym. Whatever it took, I was willing to do it.

My size wasn't going to dictate the kind of basketball player I was. No way. In fact, if my father were six-eight, my mother six-two, and the doctor told them that I might be a seven-footer, I wouldn't have approached the game any differently. I would have worked on the fundamentals like ballhandling, dribbling, shooting and free throws just the way I did work on them. And I would have paid just as much attention to all details of the game.

My advice to any young player who isn't very tall is quite simple: Play hard, believe in yourself, and don't listen to those people who try to convince you that you're doomed to fail just because you're not tall. Do what I did; use that as motivation for proving them wrong. That's always been my philosophy. At every step along the way, that's the creed I've followed: Never give up.

CHAPTER THREE

GROWING PAINS

Although basketball was my first love and the sport that occupied the majority of my time, I have to admit that I was a pretty good baseball player. My father had always felt that I was going to be a better baseball player than a basketball player and that if I had pursued it more vigorously, I had a chance to be very good.

I grew up playing baseball, beginning at the T-ball level. Mostly, I was a pitcher and a shortstop. As a pitcher, I never threw particularly hard. And I didn't throw a curve, I just threw strikes, which is always crucial, especially at that level. I had a good arm, quick hands and good hand-eye coordination, so I did OK at shortstop. Hitting is what I loved best though. I was always a good hitter. Singles and doubles, never home runs. I was a classic contact hitter in that I rarely hit for power and seldom struck out. As a freshman in high school, I led the varsity in batting with an average over .300. But baseball just wasn't fast enough for me; too many lulls in the action to suit my taste. And I have to disagree with dad—I don't think I was as good in baseball as I was in basketball. However, the main reason I gave up baseball after my sophomore year was because the two sports over- lapped and by the time basketball season was over, I'd be too far behind the other baseball players.

One thing I did like about baseball is that size isn't an issue. Nobody ever says you can't be a good baseball player just because you aren't tall. In baseball, if you can play, you can play, regardless of whether you're six-six or five-six. Size — or lack of size — doesn't present unnecessary obstacles. That's the way it should be.

Back to basketball. The first school team I actually played on was during my sixth grade year at Hanson. I had played on junior pro teams in organized leagues, but sixth grade was when I was on what I considered a real team. This was different because now we were representing our school against other county teams. Because of that, the games naturally took on much more meaning for everyone involved. Winning suddenly became far more important.

My coach that year was Ed Roberts. The first day of tryouts consisted of a one-on-one tournament among the players. Tryouts were scheduled to last for three or four days, but I played well enough to make the team after the first day. Scotty Martin, a fellow sixth-grader and my future teammate at Madisonville, made the Hanson "varsity," which was the eighth-grade team.

Until then, I had always been a starter. I'd played a lot of minutes and scored a lot of points. That's all I ever knew. Sitting on the bench wasn't something I was used to.

But that's what happened to me that year. I didn't get very much playing time at all. It was a new experience, and I didn't like it much. Whether size played a factor or not, I can't say. What I can say is that I was very disappointed.

It was tough sitting on the sidelines watching Scotty and the other guys out there playing. Tough not because I was envious of them, but because I'm such a competitor that I wanted to be out there myself, doing what I could to help the team win. Plus, I always thought I was as good as the people out there playing. As the season wore on, I became more and more upset, at the coach, at myself, at the situation. It was just an extremely difficult year for me.

After my sixth grade year, my parents decided to move me to Browning Springs, a middle school in Madisonville. They asked me if I wanted to, and after the year I'd just had, I didn't hesitate to say yes. I knew it would be a major transition for me because I'd be leaving all my old friends behind, people I'd grown up with and gone to school with from the first grade. That's always a tough thing to do, leaving old friends. But I had to look at it from another perspective: that I would have a better opportunity to get playing time at Browning Springs.

Browning Springs certainly did take some getting used to. The atmosphere there was completely different. The school was much bigger, with far more students. Suddenly, I'd gone from being someone everybody knew to just another face in the crowd. And I'd guessed correctly, I missed my old friends very much. I also guessed correctly in another area as well, I was given an opportunity to play.

Our team, which consisted of sixth, seventh and eighth graders, was exceptionally strong that year. Alan Hall was on that team. So was George Lovan. Alan was a great friend, but he was also my biggest rival. I guess that's because he was such a tremendous all-around talent. Football, baseball, basketball—he stood out in all of them. I used to compare myself to him. I wanted to be as good as he was.

I was a starting guard on that Browning Springs team. After getting virtually no playing time the year before at Hanson, I guess I felt a certain sense of vindication. Here I was, not only playing, but starting on a team loaded with talented players. It was a terrific feeling.

Sitting on the bench as a sixth grader at Hanson caused me to question my own ability. For the first time in my life, my confidence was shaken. I was sitting on the sidelines, wondering just how good I really was. Then as a seventh grader, I started and played a lot of minutes for a really good team. I was the key man on the team. It was just totally different. I was starting on the best team in the county, yet I hadn't been good enough to even play for Hanson the year before.

The playoffs at the end of that year turned out to be the crowning moment for me. We played at the Earlington Junior High gym. After winning our first game, we played Hanson in the semifinal round. Hanson versus Browning Springs. The gym was packed. I would be playing against my former teammates. I'd also be playing in front of many adults who resented me for switching schools. I had never been so pumped up, so psyched for a game in my life. I wanted to win, and I wanted to play well. And that's what happened. We won rather easily, and I had a great game. The next night, Alan, Jeff White and I each scored nine points as we beat Nortonville 39-37 to win the county championship. Hollywood's best writers couldn't have written a more perfect script.

What I was too young to know at the time was that those Hollywood writers keep on writing, and that sometimes Act II isn't as pleasant as Act I. Sometimes, in fact, Act II turns out to be a tragedy.

My parents and I had often discussed the possiblity of holding me back a year in school. In this case, if we chose to do it, I would be a seventh grader for a second straight year. This is something that is done all the time by athletes all around the country. Sometimes it's even done by non-athletes. Essentially, what it does is allow you time to grow and mature, both mentally and physically. That's the positive side. The negative side is that you aren't eligible to compete in athletics for that year.

We talked about it over the summer, never comitting one way or the other. In the end, however, the decision to hold back was practically made for us.

I was having some really bad knee problems at the time. I had a bone disease that was causing excruciating pain in both knees. One doctor told me to stay out of sports for two years; that was the only thing you could do for it. Other doctors told us different things, none of which were acceptable. Then we went to a doctor in Nashville who knew immediately what was wrong—not enough blood was getting to the bone. He said surgery would remedy the problem. Believe it or not, that was good news. Given the choice of surgery or not playing basketball for two years, I'll take surgery anytime.

Our decision was made; I would repeat the seventh grade. Fortunately, an accelerated learning program began that year, and since I made good grades, I was eligible to participate. That meant I wasn't repeating the same classes, even though I was repeating the same grade. That eliminated the classroom boredom I'd feared.

The doctor decided to operate on one knee in August and the second knee in January. The first operation required him to actually open up the knee, go in and drill the bone in four places. That was the tough one. The second knee only needed arthroscopic surgery, which isn't nearly so painful.

I was on crutches for much of that year. It was a very uncomfortable time for me. After the first operation, the doctor told me to take it easy for three or four weeks, to refrain from doing anything even remotely strenuous. Naturally, I couldn't wait that long. Anytime I was in the gym, I would pick up a basketball and try to dribble it or shoot it. I couldn't curb those natural instincts, even when I was hobbling around on crutches.

Sitting out that year was one of the toughest things I've ever done. I missed the competition like crazy, I missed getting out there on the court and I missed playing in the games. I am not a very good spectator.

I occupied my time watching my Browning Springs teammates play and going to Madisonville's varsity games. If I couldn't play, at least I could be around it. But even that was painful because I couldn't sit for long periods of time. Bending my knee hurt too much, so I had to watch much of the game standing up.

Because of the surgery, I always considered my eighth grade year as a comeback of sorts. Anytime you start playing again after having had surgery, especially a serious knee operation, you can't help but wonder if you're the same player as before. There are always doubts, and they aren't laid aside until you actually test yourself on the field of battle. I was lucky. I not only passed the test, I passed it with flying colors. In fact, my eighth-grade year proved to be perhaps the most pivotal year in my life.

Repeating a grade meant that all of my friends had now passed me by. I was still going to be in junior high, while my teammates were now in high school. However, from a basketball standpoint, I didn't think that should matter. Just because they were a year ahead of me in the classroom didn't mean they were that much better than me on the court. I wasn't being cocky. I'd held my own with them two years earlier, so why I couldn't I do it now?

I went to Coach Don Parson and asked him if I could try out for the freshman team. He knew me from junior high and from his camp, so he said sure. I went out and made the team. Now, all of a sudden, I'm back playing with Scotty and Greg Fairrow and all those other guys. It was just like old times. Except for one thing—logistics. I was still at the middle school and the varsity practiced at the high school. So, each day, as soon as classes were over, I'd get on the bus and ride across town for practice. It was a hectic setup, but I didn't mind at all. I was just thrilled to be on the team that I would have traveled any distance in order to play.

Jim Martin was the freshman coach and one of the greatest guys I know. He really did a lot to help me, spending extra time teaching me all phases of the game. Coach Martin is one of those people who, after you have some success, you look back and realize how important he was to your development.

Moving up was a big test for me, and early on, I didn't handle it all that well. The season was about to begin, and I was struggling in a big way. I was maybe the seventh or eighth guy on the team. But once the season started, my game really picked up. I can't explain why, but it did. Maybe it just took me a while to shake off the rust that accumulates during a time of inactivity.

Whatever the reason, things fell into place for me. I earned a starting spot after just a couple of games. I played so well, in fact, that I was moved up to the junior varsity. In my first JV game, I came in, made a couple of steals and hit a couple of layups. I played exceptionally well, probably much better than anyone expected, including myself.

Later on in the season, I was moved up to the varsity. Talk about being thrilled. I was an eighth-grader playing for the Madisonville Maroons; playing for Don Parson, a coaching legend in Kentucky high school basketball ranks. I'd sure come a long way from Hanson in a very short period of time.

Don't get me wrong, I didn't see much playing time. Most of the time, I'd sit on the end of the bench talking to Skip McGaw. He was the only sophomore on the team, and he wasn't getting much PT either. We got to know each other quite well during that time. Skip would become an outstanding player for the Maroons. He and I had some memorable times together. We also won a lot of games together. Later, Skip would walk on at UK and play for Coach Pitino's first team there.

When you move up as fast as I did, you always wonder if it causes any resentment among your friends. Probably, it does. It's never easy when you see younger guys pass you up. Remember, I had some resentment during my last year at Hanson. I guess it's just human nature. I will say this: If any of my teammates were resentful, they didn't show it.

From my perspective, I couldn't worry about it. My feeling has always been that if I played well, if I proved that I belonged, then I didn't care what anybody else said. Even now, the only people I want to please are my coaches and my parents. If I make them happy, chances are I'm doing things well. I've had games where I scored a lot of points and the fans thought I was terrific, yet the truth is, I was lousy. I knew it, the coaches knew it and my father knew it. He knew I didn't have to score 30 points a night in order to play well. He knew when I played well and when I played poorly.

The scorebook is a bad place to look for performance.

CHAPTER FOUR

PREP DREAMS AND SWEET 16 NIGHTMARES

If I had to describe my high school career at Madisonville in a single word, it would be storybook. I had the kind of career that very few athletes are fortunate enough to have. I played at a great school, for a highly respected coach, with a bunch of really terrific teammates. Those were special times in my life, times I'll never forget. It was just a lot of fun.

The four men most responsible for the success I've achieved as a basketball player are my father, Don Parson, Norm Stewart and Rick Pitino. Not surprisingly, all four are similar in many ways: they know the game of basketball, they demand your absolute best effort, and they treat you in a fair and impartial manner. As a player, you can't ask for more than that.

I knew about Coach Parson a long time before I actually played for him. I first met him when I was very young, probably no older than seven or eight. It was during his summer basketball camp that I always attended. He's one of those coaches whose reputation precedes him, and when I met him, I understood why. He has the reputation of being a very tough disciplinarian.

When you play for him, you quickly learn that his reputation is fact, not fiction.

Playing for Coach Parson was a blessing for me, not only because he taught me a lot and because he gave me an opportunity, but because he never let me get carried away with myself. He kept me in line. I don't mean to say that I was ever a problem, but let's face it, when you score a bunch of points, or read your name in the paper all the time, it's easy to get a little too full of yourself. Take my word for it, that never happened to me. My parents and Coach Parson weren't about to let my head get too big.

I had played a little on the varsity during my eighth-grade year, but I didn't get many minutes. That taste of varsity experience was all I needed to drive me toward becoming a better basketball player. I desperately wanted to start as a freshman, and, even though there were several players I would have to beat out, I knew I had a chance to do it. That's all I thought about, making the first five. I viewed it as another big challenge, so I worked extremely hard that summer, and by the time practice started I had improved my game tremendously. The hard work and extra effort paid off too, because when we opened the season, I was the starting point guard.

We weren't expected to be particularly strong that season. We were young, inexperienced and not very big. Our center, Jerome Rickard, was only six-four or six-five. Jimmy Corneal, a senior, had been around for several years so he was the team leader. Mainly, though, we had a lot of young guys who were called upon to play key roles, guys like Chris Bowles and Alan Bearman and me, all five-feet-seven inches of me.

Anyway, no one expected much from us that year, but we proved them wrong by having an excellent season, finishing with a final record of 20-8. Considering the schedule we played, and the fact that we played in the second region (which is, I think, year after year the toughest region in the state) a 20-8 record is outstanding.

I can still remember my first game as a starter, how excited and nervous I was. We played Apollo which meant Rex

Chapman. Think about that, your first time out of the gate and you've got to deal with Rex Chapman, one of the four or five best high school players in the country. Plus, they had another great guard in Greg Baughn. Talk about a challenge for a rookie; try dealing with that backcourt duo.

We played them tough, but in the end, Rex was just too much for us. He scored 25, and they spoiled our season opener by beating us 73-68. I think I played fairly well, scoring 14 in my varsity debut. But we didn't win the game, so I wasn't satisfied. I hate losing, and no matter how many points I score in a losing effort, nothing takes away the bitter taste in my mouth or the knot in my stomach. Individual achievement cannot remedy the pain of defeat.

A few weeks later, Jimmy Corneal scored 25 points to help us hold off Union County 69-66. That was a big win because it was Coach Parson's 500th career victory as a head coach. After the game, the school gave him 500 balloons with a dollar bill in each one. He's had a lot of great teams at Madisonville North. I was just proud to be a part of the one that got him his 500th win.

I always admired the courage of this team. We showed that bravery in our own invitational tournament, which we won despite being at less than full strength. In the first game against Franklin-Simpson, we were down 24-5, then came back to win 64-60. The next night, we beat University Heights 70-67 in overtime to win the championship. This victory was especially impressive because Corneal was out with a foot injury, Alan Bearman and Scotty Martin were out with the flu, and Skip McGaw was playing with a broken nose.

I scored 30 points for the first time in a varsity game against Hopkinsville. I was red-hot that night. Unfortunately, we couldn't stop LaMont Ware. He scored 31, and they beat us 74-69. There was that bitter taste again.

We beat South Hopkins 58-50 and Dawson Springs 77-61 to win the district championship. Chris Bowles, John Perdue and I were named to the all-tournament team.

Winning the district was a big thrill for all of us. Sure,

Madisonville is expected to win the district tournament every year, but being expected to win and actually winning are two different things. Nobody gives you anything. You have to earn it on the field of battle. We earned it, and for most of the guys on that team, it was our first chance to cut down the nets, something a lot of other great Madisonville players had done in the past. We were proud to continue that tradition of winning.

As I said earlier, the second region is consistently the toughest in the state. Christian County, Hopkinsville, Madisonville, Henderson County, UHA, Union County: those teams are always loaded with great athletes. And every year, you can count on another couple of teams being really strong. It's that way every year. It was when I played, and it still is today.

Hopkinsville was a heavy favorite to win the regional my freshman year, but we felt we had a legitimate shot at winning it. We'd played them close during the regular season, so we knew we could compete with them. To make matters even better, we drew in opposite brackets. Maybe someone else would get lucky and knock them off. We weren't above hoping for some outside help.

We opened against Lyon County, and, although they gave us a scare, we managed to put them away 74-62. I had a good game, finishing with 26 points. Jerome Rickard also came up big, scoring 18.

That win put us against UHA, a team we'd beaten in OT during the regular season. We lost in the regional 71-61, but what I remember most about that game isn't that our dream of making it to the Sweet 16 had been crushed, but a rather bizarre incident that occurred during half-time.

Our assistant principal came into the dressing room and just started yelling at the team, saying that I was the only one who was playing hard and that everybody else needed to start picking it up. It was wild. This guy didn't have anything to do with basketball, he'd never been in the dressing room before, yet here he was, screaming and yelling like crazy. None of us knew what to think. Neither did Coach Parson. He just let the guy keep on talking.

The truth is, UHA had a very good team. We were outmanned. So losing, painful as it was, was not a surprise.

I made the all-tournament team, which was a nice way to end what had been a surprisingly successful season. But it wasn't what I really wanted. I wanted to make it to the Sweet 16. All of us did. And we knew that with the players we had coming back next year, we'd stand an excellent chance of getting there.

Our expectations for the sophomore season were completely different from the previous year. This time, everyone figured we'd have a strong club. Bowles, Bearman, Perdue, Scotty Martin and Skip were back, along with Willie Liles and Herb Arnarson, a foreign exchange student from Iceland. That was a very talented team, a very tall team.

We opened the season by beating Apollo 78-62 (Rex had graduated, thank goodness) and then winning the Graves County Tip-Off Classic. We won our first six before Warren Central upset us 62-44. Two games after that loss we bounced back to beat Hopkinsville 78-66. I had 27 in that game and Bearman added 16.

One of the highlights of that season was when we beat No. 2-ranked Owensboro 62-61. I sat out that game because of a sprained ankle, but the guys stepped it up and won without me. That proved we weren't a one-man team, as some people seemed to believe. All the guys on this team could play.

We finished the regular season with a 21-4 record, then marched through the district tourney, easily beating South Hopkins 95-54 and West Hopkins 96-71. I scored 32 in the championship game, and was named to the all-tourney team, along with Chris Bowles and Scotty Martin.

The regional was held at our gym, which was a big advantage for us. It also gave us an extra incentive to win: what could be sweeter than earning a trip to the state tournament by winning the regional on your own home court?

We beat Henderson County 56-52 in a real nail-biter. I always enjoyed playing against Henderson County because I have such great respect for their coach, Curtis Turley. He's a good friend of mine. His teams are always difficult to beat, and that was sure the case that night.

The next night, I scored 27 and John Perdue had 14 and we beat Livingston Central 59-48. That put us in the championship game against Caldwell County, which was led by Michael Gray, an All-Stater.

We were one win away from realizing the dream that every Kentucky high school basketball player has from the first day he begins playing — to play in the Sweet 16. One victory away. Only thirty-two minutes. I've never been more nervous.

Caldwell County had beaten us earlier that year in a very close game. I hit a shot from half-court that would have given us the victory, but the referees said it didn't count. Now, in the regional final, we had an extra reason to play hard: revenge.

It was another close game, but this time the good guys came out on top. I had 16, Skip and Chris had 10 apiece, and we won 55-47. We were going to the Sweet 16!

It's hard to describe the feeling you have when you know you're going to the state tournament for the first time as a player. I'd been to the Sweet 16 many times as a spectator and I'd always envied those players. Now, here I was, going to the big show as a player. It was a tremendous accomplishment for all of us, and a great thrill.

The first thing I remember thinking when the final buzzer sounded was that we were going to Rupp Arena. We'd be playing where the Kentucky Wildcats play. I'd never played in Rupp before, so that added to the excitement.

We were paired against Owensboro in the opening round. The Red Devils were ranked No. 1 in the state. We weren't scared by that ranking. Why should we be? We'd already beaten them during the regular season, and I didn't play in that game. I think every player on our team genuinely felt that we had a good shot at winning the state championship. And we might have if I'd just kept my mouth shut.

After we won the regional against Caldwell County, a reporter came up to me and said, "Your team has already beaten

Owensboro without you. What do you think you're going to do this time?"

Well, like an idiot, I said we weren't going to have much trouble with them. My exact quote was that "we were going to beat them even worse." Of course, that quote was the next day's headline in the newspaper.

So we get to the state tourney and, when we went out to the center circle for the opening tip, the Owensboro guys came up to me and said, "OK, let's see if you beat us worse now."

They were on me like glue the whole game. Everywhere I went, there was at least one Red Devil defender in my face. I hit just 2 of 14 field goal attempts and finished with only five points. I had a sore throat that day, and afterward, some people wanted to use that as an excuse for my poor performance. But I played badly because Owensboro made me play badly. The other guys on the team played well —Skip had a excellent game—but Owensboro beat us 55-48.

I was disappointed because we lost, but more so because I felt I had let my team down. The loss bothered me much more than my poor performance did because I really thought we could go far in that tournament. Losing in the first round was a bitter pill to swallow.

I learned a big lesson from that experience — keep your mouth shut and just play the game. Don't ever give additional ammunition to the enemy by saying something dumb, like I did. I'd spoken in haste, and although what I said wasn't in any way meant to put down Owensboro, my statement backfired. My words came back to haunt me. That was my first experience with the press and it taught me to handle media situations carefully.

We finished with a final record of 26-5, and I ended up with a scoring average of 17.7 points per game. To my surprise, I received several post-season honors: third-team All-State by The Louisville Courier-Journal and The Associated Press, and honorable mention All-State in USA Today.

The big change that took place between my sophomore and junior seasons was the addition of the three-point shot. That had a big effect on the game. It was certainly a big advantage for me: I could always shoot the ball from very far out. Because of that, I didn't have to alter my game at all. If anything, I probably scooted in a few inches.

The three-point shot was a big weapon for our team during my junior season. Quite a few of our players were good outside shooters, so it helped us a lot. Scotty Martin hit about as many three-pointers as I did.

There was nowhere for us to hide when that season rolled around. We weren't going to sneak up and beat anyone. In the preseason polls we were ranked third in the state and first in the region, and I was rated fourth behind Richie Farmer, Allan Houston and Scott Boley.

Expectations were high all the way around that year. I felt a little pressure, but not a whole lot. More than anything, I felt good about that team. We had a ton of talent coming back, so I couldn't help but feel positive. Chris Bowles and Alan Bearman were both seniors and they were six-nine and six-eight, respectively. Scotty was back, I was back, Herb Arnarson, who was six-five, was back, and James Marsh, also six-five, joined the team after moving to Madisonville from Germany, where his father had been stationed in the service. In every way, this was an exceptionally strong basketball team.

Another big change that season was that we were allowed to play in some out-of-state tournaments. Prior to that year, the school board wouldn't let us take part in those tournaments. They didn't want us missing school, or they didn't think we could come up with the money to finance the trips. Whatever their reasoning, they always vetoed it. My sophomore year, we had been invited to a couple of tournaments, but the school board had said no.

However, during my junior year, they changed their minds and said we could pick one tournament and they'd let us participate in it. Since we had such a strong team that year, we had invitations to several tournaments around the country. We decided to play in the Great Florida Shootout in Kissimee.

That was an incredible tournament, it was loaded with so many great teams and so many outstanding players. We knew it was going to be a huge challenge for us, especially since we had to play without Chris Bowles, who was out with a broken wrist. But if you're a competitor, and if you want to improve, you have to play against the best teams and the top individuals. You can't know if you're progressing or standing still unless you constantly test yourself.

I scored 29 points in an 82-50 first-round win over Trumann, Arkansas. That win improved our record to 6-0 and set us up for a second-round game against Miami Senior High School. Where were they rated? No. 1 in the nation, that's all.

That Miami Senior team had Cesar Portillo, Doug Edwards, Jose Ramos, and a tall, skinny sophomore with a large nose named Gimel. That's right, my future UK teammate, Gimel Martinez. We played a great game. Both teams played well, for that matter. And we had them beat right up until the end. We were going up against a front line that was seven-two, six-nine and six-eight, and we had to do it without Chris, who was, in my opinion, the best center in Kentucky at the time. We were hitting threes like crazy, really hustling, and with four minutes left, we were leading by six points. Then we just wore out. They eventually came back to beat us 76-70. Scotty Martin had a monster game, scoring 26 points. I finished with 22.

Near the end of the game, there was this big bench-clearing brawl. I don't know what started the fight, but it was a pretty good one. I think we were just so tight for the game, and they were getting upset because this little team from Kentucky was giving them all they could handle. We weren't going to back down from anybody. Neither were they. So tempers just flared.

To this day, Gimel and I still dog each other about that game. The strange thing is, his story keeps changing over the years. When I first came to UK, he was always telling me how we came in and almost beat them. Now, as the years have gone by, he says they beat us by 20 and that it wasn't even close. I think Gimel is losing his memory.

After we beat Jacksonville Ribault 83-78 (I had 31 points, Herb Arnarson had 22), we went up against Gulfport High School. That meant I would be facing Chris Jackson, probably the best high school guard in America at the time. I'd heard of him, but I really didn't know that much about him. It didn't take me long to learn all I'd ever want to know. You've heard that joke about someone scoring six points before the national anthem ended. It was that way with Chris.

He had about 30 points in the first half, and eventually ended up with 48. It was unbelievable; we couldn't do anything to stop him. I don't think he even played in the fourth quarter. He was easily the best player I ever played against in high school. Early on, he and I were trading baskets, but in the end, they were way too much for us. We lost 94-75.

Later that season, we played another of the country's top-rated teams, fifth-ranked Vashon High of St. Louis. We had an open date and were looking to get a highly ranked team to come to our place for a game, so Coach Parson scheduled them. The game was sold out two weeks before we played. People were standing up along the rails. The place was packed.

The guys from Vashon came in with fancy warm-ups, carrying fancy traveling bags. Most people didn't give us much of a chance to win but we did. We upset them 68-56. We led the entire game, and ended up winning pretty handily. That win was a big boost for our team. It gave us a lot of confidence. After the game, Vashon's coach said some really nice things about us. That turned out to be their only loss all season. They went on to win the Missouri state championship.

Personally, I think that was my best game overall during my high school career. Points, assists, handling the ball, running the team, I don't think I ever played a more complete game. And we won, which allowed me to enjoy it even more.

After that win, we went to No. 2 in the state, which is where we stayed until tournament time came around.

The district tournament was little more than a tune-up for the regional. We crushed South Hopkins 75-38 and West

Hopkins 87-48 to win the title again. Marsh, Herb Arnarson, Bowles and I made the all-tournament team.

At the time, we were expected to contend for the state championship, which meant that we were big favorites to win the regional. Even though we were playing awfully well at the time, we knew it wasn't going to be easy. Nothing ever comes easy in the second region.

We had no problem with Trigg County in the opener, winning 86-45. That game bothered me some, because we won so easily. I was concerned we might become overconfident. Looming ahead was Hopkinsville in the semifinals and Christian County in the championship game (if we got there), and both of those teams were capable of beating us.

I shot the lights out against Hoptown, scoring 30 points to help us come away with a 76-63 win. Herb and Chris also played very well, scoring 16 and 14 points.

Christian County was led by Chris Whitney, who is currently playing for the San Antonio Spurs in the NBA. He was a really tough basketball player. He had a big first half, but we held him scoreless in the final two quarters, and that proved to be the deciding factor. Thanks to a balanced scoring attack, we won the game — and our second straight regional crown — by a score of 67-51. James Marsh and I each had 17 points, while Herb Arnarson and Chris Bowles had 16 apiece.

It's a great feeling to know that you've lived up to expectations. There's tremendous pressure on you when you're ranked No. 1. There's nowhere to go but down. So you do have a strong sense of pride when you know you've handled all the hurdles and fulfilled your potential.

We went to the state tournament in Freedom Hall confident that we could come home with the big prize. But it didn't turn out like we'd hoped. Instead, for the second straight year, we came home with our tails tucked firmly between our legs and disappointment on our faces.

And what made it even worse for us is that the situation was almost exactly like the previous year, even down to the home town of the school that beat us. The previous year, it had been Owensboro Senior; this year, it was Apollo. We had beaten Apollo 71-60 in the regular season. We had no trouble with them, really. Yet, we get to Freedom Hall, when it really counts, and they beat us 73-62 in overtime. I scored 14 points, but that's about all I can say. For the second straight year, I was something less than outstanding in the Sweet 16.

I think the reason why we lost is the oldest reason of all — we simply overlooked them. We didn't take care of business. We were the better team, but being better is no guarantee of success. You have to play better, and we didn't.

If fulfilling expectations is the best feeling, then losing a game you should have won is the worst. I know I felt terrible after that loss. We all felt that way. I think we were beginning to wonder if perhaps we were doomed when it came to the Sweet 16. Two straight trips, two straight first-round losses to teams we'd already beaten. It was very frustrating for all of us.

One of the sad realities of sports is that the majority of teams end their season on a down note. Only the champion ends with a victory. For everyone else, the final game goes in the L column. That has a way of dulling the light of your successes. We had a 29-4 record, were ranked as high as second in the state, won the district and the regional, yet all we could remember was that loss to Apollo. Only after the passage of time can you stand back, look at what happened, and say, "We did all right."

I know it was that way for me as well. I averaged 22 points per game and was named first-team All-State, but those honors, nice as they were, couldn't take away the sting of losing. Looking at it now, I'm very proud to have made first-team All-State. It's a tremendous honor. It made me feel good because I was there with people like Richie Farmer and Allan Houston, two guys who were not only great players but also great friends.

A lot of my success had to do with my team. I was playing with such great players that it was easy for me to do well. Whatever success I achieved is directly related to the generosity of my teammates at Madisonville. I am greatly indebted to them.

In a strange way, my senior season was much the same as my freshman year, especially in the pre-season. For the most part, no one figured us to be among the stronger teams in the state. We'd lost four starters to graduation and our starting center, Randy Green, was the quarterback on the football team, which meant he'd be joining us late.

Herb Arnarson and I were the only returning players with much experience. We were also the players who would have to shoulder much of the scoring load. The rest of the guys were role players. I think what made that team so good was that every player understood and accepted his designated role. Randy Green absolutely loved to get in there and rebound. He was a rebounding machine who didn't care if he ever scored a point. Theron Pearson was an excellent shooter, and Jimmy Dodd was there to play great defense.

You can look at our first three games that year and know that my role was to score. I had 34, 29 and 38 in those three games. There was more pressure on me to score, no question about that. But that didn't bother me. My teammates knew it as well. If we were going to win, I was going to have to score a lot of points. So was Herb. Because of that, my teammates were always looking to get me open, always looking to get me the ball. There was not any jealousy on their part, or any hot dog attitude on my part. It was simply the way things had to be if we wanted to be successful.

One of the most exciting games I ever played in — and one of the biggest upsets I've had during my career — came when we knocked off No. 1-ranked Louisville Ballard 99-93 in the first round of the King of the Bluegrass Tournament in Louisville. That matchup wasn't an accident, either. When we found out that we'd be playing Ballard, we knew exactly what the tourney officials had done: set me up against Allan Houston, the No. 1 player in the state.

Ballard was loaded that year. Along with Allan, they had Mark Bell and Kenneth Martin, two players who went on to have outstanding college careers. We went into that game thinking we had nothing to lose. We got Allan into early foul trouble, which was one of the big reasons we were able to win. He still managed to score 35, but Herb had 34 and I had 32, and that was enough to offset Allan. Beating Ballard gave us a big lift and a big boost of confidence.

After we beat Central City 71-51 in the second round, we had to go up against another strong Louisville team with a great player. This time it was Louisville Central and Dwayne Morton, who went on to do so well at the University of Louisville.

During that game, which we won 89-82 in overtime, we ran a set play that freed me up just beyond the three-point line. I was able to make it work by hitting four straight treys. I had 44 points that night, my career high. Dwayne had 38 for Central.

In the championship game, we went against Christ the King from New York City. They were ranked fifth in the country and were led by Jamal Faulkner and Khalid Reeves. I had 24 in the first half, but right before half-time, I got knocked unconscious. We were right there with them until midway in the third quarter, then they pulled away. They were just too big and too strong for us. The final score was 96-84. I had 35 for us, but Faulkner had 32 and Reeves had 31 for them.

One thing I'll say about our team my senior year is that we played against the best. And we always acquitted ourselves very well. Later that year, we played in the King Cotton Invitational in Pine Bluff, Arkansas. We beat Memphis Westwood, lost to Archbishop Shaw, then beat Wehrle High School out of Columbus, Ohio. Archbishop Shaw had Melvin Simon and Wehrle had Lawrence Funderburke, who was a very close friend of mine. In the loss to Archbishop Shaw, I broke the tournament record by scoring 37 points. A nice accomplishment, but once again, a loss kept me from enjoying it.

I was really looking forward to playing against Lawrence, but it didn't happen. He was suspended from the team right before the game, and ended up quitting. He was in my room the night before it all happened. We talked about it for a long time. I don't know all the details, but I do know that he and his coach didn't get along very well. It was a bad situation for everyone. Lawrence is a misunderstood individual. That's too bad, because he's actually a very nice person. Maybe he's made some poor choices or bad decisions, but I know he has a good heart. He hasn't deserved much of the bad press he's gotten over the years.

Late in the season, just a week or so before tournament time, our team, which no one took seriously at the beginning of the year, jumped to No. 2 behind Clay County in the ratings. We had really surprised everyone, including ourselves.

We again won the district without much trouble, then went to the regional, where we played three absolutely magnificent games. Talk about peaking at the right time. Everything was clicking for us. Defense, offense, everything. We had never been better.

Crittenden County was our first victim. We beat them 98-54. I had 24 points and 15 assists, but it was Theron Pearson who stood out that night, scoring 28 points for us. The next night, I had 33 and Herb had 23 and we again won easily, this time beating Union County 106-74. You usually don't win games so convincingly in the second region tournament, but like I said, we were on fire.

Hopkinsville was our opponent in the championship game. I had never been more pumped up for a game than I was for that one. It was my senior year, and it was now or never as far as getting back to the state tournament and proving that Madisonville could do well there. I also wanted another chance to prove that I wasn't one of those players who couldn't perform in the big games.

Luckily, we came out and put together another great effort. We won 92-82. I had 37 and Herb had 26. If a team caught Herb and me hot on the same night, they just weren't going to beat us. That's what happened that night. We both hit the bucket.

Prior to the season, not many people gave us a chance to make it back to the Sweet 16, yet here we were, going back for the third straight year. That's what made it so special. The win over Hoptown was also special was because it was Coach Parson's

600th career victory. We were all extremely happy for him because he was big reason why this team had overachieved. I was with Coach Parson when he won number 500 and number 600, which means I was around for a long time. I'm sure Coach Parson probably thought I'd been around forever.

Maybe the third time is a charm because I finally had a good game in the state tournament. We beat Prestonsburg 76-65, and I had 39 points. In that game, I hit seven of nine three-pointers. Herb also played well, scoring 23. Like I said, when he and I were both on, we were a tough team to beat. I came out determined to have a good game. I'd made up my mind to relax, get into a rhythm and put the ball up as much as I could. I wasn't going to worry about what had happened the previous two years.

Our win, and my own performance, made me feel good because it proved that we could actually win a game in the state tournament. It also calmed me down for the next game, which was against Marshall County, a team we had beaten by 22 points in the regular season. I'd scored 36 points in that game.

Despite having beaten them earlier, I wasn't about to overlook them. That's because of their coach, Allan Hatcher. He's a great coach. And they had some solid players like Dan Hall and Aaron Beth. If that weren't enough to keep us from overlooking Marshall County, all we had to do was remember what had happened during the past two state tournaments. We didn't want that to happen again.

But it did. Although we led for much of the game, they ended up beating us 69-66. I scored 26 points in that game, but all I can remember is the three-pointer I took at the buzzer that rimmed out.

Coach Parson was pretty upset with the officiating that day. We had six more field goals than Marshall County, but they shot 30 free throws to our 13. I think that's why he was so angry. Second region teams often go to the charity stripe on fewer occasions than their opponents in the state tournament. I think there's a reason for that. Second region officials really allow a physical game. They let you bang and knock pretty good. Like the college game, really. Then when second region teams get to the state tournament where officials tend to call it close, they get hit with a bunch of fouls. I know that's happened to several Madisonville teams in the past.

I can remember standing on the Rupp Arena floor for a couple of minutes, looking around, thinking about how my career at North was over and about all the great times I had there. I didn't worry too much about that loss. Instead, I concentrated on the good games I'd had, the great teams I'd been a part of, all the great teammates I'd been fortunate enough to play with, what a great year we'd had, and how much I had enjoyed playing for Coach Parson. It bothered me that we didn't beat Marshall County, but I wasn't about to let it diminish the pride I felt about what I'd been able to do at North. After the game, my dad came into the dressing room and told me how proud he was of what I'd done and how I'd handled myself. Hearing that from him made me feel especially good.

That team finished with a 30-5 record. I've always said it was my most satisfying year. There was great pressure on me to succeed, to score and to run the team. I had a lot on my shoulders, yet I still managed to average 32.2 points per game. But it was just so much fun playing on that team. Everybody contributed. Jeff Duvall would come in and give us a big lift with a three. Randy Green, who could have been a great scorer, was willing to limit himself to being mostly a rebounder. It was just a great team to be part of. A lot of great honors came my way after the season; being voted first-team All-State, being named to the Parade All-America team, and being chosen to play in several all-star games. All of that was nice, but for me, the biggest honor came when the school retired my uniform jersey, No. 20. That came as a big surprise to me. They did it at the basketball banquet. Coach Parson got up on the podium and started talking about me and some of my accomplishments. Then he announced that they were retiring my jersey. I was only the second Madisonville player to have his jersey retired. Frank Ramsey was the first. That's pretty good company to be keeping. Needless to say, it was a very emotional moment for me.

Another accomplishment I'm extremely proud of is being the all-time leading scorer at Madisonville with 2,676 points. Not that I'm hung up about points, it's not that at all. But scoring that many points is a testament to consistency and stamina. It means I did the job night after night. Consistency is what every athlete strives for. The night I broke the record was really weird. And it didn't happen on the night when everyone tried to help me get the record. It came one game later.

I had no idea that I was even close to it. I didn't even know what the record was, or who held it. I later found out that it was held by Jim Mitchell. Anyway, there were three minutes left in the game and I needed three points to get it. Coach Parson called a time out and told everyone what the situation was, and for them to keep feeding me the ball. Everytime down the court, my teammates would get me the ball and I'd put up a shot. I wasn't even getting close to making a basket. I was pressing so bad that it was affecting my shot. So, what happened? I didn't break the record that night. I broke it early in the next game. When I did, they stopped the game and gave me the game ball. I went up into the stands and gave it to my mom. That was a big moment for me.

I can't imagine anyone having a better or a more enjoyable high school career than I had. I was very lucky. But it was a chapter that had ended; it was now time to move on. Ahead was a busy summer. Then college. I couldn't wait.

CHAPTER FIVE

BURT REYNOLDS AND A BUSY SIGNAL

Being recruited to play major college basketball is really a heady experience. Here you are, 17 or 18 years old and you're getting calls and letters from the most famous and successful coaches in the college ranks. It's a dizzying time for the athlete and his family. It's also a very serious time because there's so much at stake. You want to choose a college where you'll be happy, where you can get a good education, where you'll be treated fairly and where, hopefully, you can get some quality playing time. With so many important factors involved, it's not an easy decision to make.

I was luckier than most high school players because my father had been a coach and was very familiar with the whole recruiting process. That helped me a lot, especially in the beginning. When I started getting a few letters during my sophomore year, he was quick to tell me that they didn't mean anything. Everybody gets letters. He kept telling me that I had to go out and prove myself on the court. He also kept me from getting the big-head. My mom was also very supportive. She just kept telling me to keep working hard and everything would work out fine.

One thing my parents made clear from the beginning was that they weren't going to make my decision for me. They helped me see the pros and cons of each situation, and they answered any questions I had, but they were never biased toward any particular school. They went with me when I made a couple of unofficial visits, but they never pushed me in any direction. Since I would have to live with whatever decision I made, they wanted me to make it on my own.

I'd say the recruiting first started in the middle of my junior year. That's when coaches started coming to watch me play. The first coach I can remember was Arizona assistant Kevin O'Neill, who's now the head coach at Tennessee. Virginia was really following me by then. So was Florida State. The way it turned out, the main schools that ended up recruiting me the hardest were the ones that recruited me the earliest.

At the beginning it wasn't a hassle at all. In fact, I was excited by it. Being recruited to play college basketball was something I'd always wanted and now it was happening. I enjoyed it. Here were all these big-time schools coming to watch me play. How could I not enjoy it? Sure, sometimes if I had a bad practice or a bad game, and then one of the coaches called, I might not feel like talking to him. But that's about the only time it bothered me. Mostly, I enjoyed the phone calls. I loved talking to all the coaches.

Things really began to intensify during the summer before my senior year. I went to several camps, like the Nike camp, and, of course, all the big-time coaches were there watching us play. By then, I pretty much knew which schools really wanted me and which ones were uncertain about me or didn't want me.

I don't think there's any doubt that I felt much more pressure during those camps than I did at any other time during the entire recruiting process. I think it's that way for most players. There is an extreme amount of pressure on you, because a lot of times, a camp can make you or break you. What's scary is that there are certain individuals who aren't coaches — the so-called recruiting "gurus" — who have an enormous amount of influence. If you go and have a bad camp, and if those gurus put out the word that you can't play, it might keep certain college coaches from giving you a serious look. Also, if a coach is there seeing you for the first time, and you don't perform well, it's going to put a bad impression in his mind. So you are under pressure to do well. However, the way I look at it is, hey, if you can't play well against the best, then the big-time coaches shouldn't be interested in you.

When I went to the camps, I always tried to follow my mom's advice: play as hard as I could and everything would fall into place. That's a piece of wisdom that has helped me throughout my career.

I played really well that summer, which helped raise my stock quite a bit. I made a good showing at Nike against all the best players in the country, then I had some excellent games while playing for my father's all-star team during tournaments in Lexington and Las Vegas. By the end of that summer, I think I had proved to everyone that I could play, and succeed, at the major college level.

Since I knew I could only make five visits, it was important that I whittle the list down immediately, which I did right before the start of my senior year. I think it's a major advantage to cut it down to five as quickly as possible. If you do like some guys are doing these days, have a list of 10 or 12 schools, all you're going to do is get confused. You won't be able to determine who is who after a while. Only after you cut it down can you really start to study the pros and cons of each school.

If you can, I think it's a good idea to commit early. That way, you put it behind you and it doesn't affect your play. You have to remember that you aren't the only player on the team. If you're distracted, or if you don't play up to your potential because outside factors are interfering with your focus, it affects your teammates as well. One thing you should never forget is that the better the team does, the better you do as an individual. I know I never forgot that. I was well aware that by playing in the state tournament as a sophomore and as a junior, my chances of being recruited were greatly increased. And I couldn't have played in the Sweet 16 if it weren't for my teammates. I don't care how big a star you are, in a team sport like basketball, you can't reach the top by yourself.

That's the main reason why I decided to commit early. Quite a few college coaches were coming around to watch our practices and our games, and I didn't want their presence to affect me or my teammates. If I'm on the court but worried about the coaches in the stands, or if my teammates are worried, it might hurt the team. I certainly didn't want that to happen. So I just thought it was best for everyone's sake to get it out of the way as soon as possible.

I'll tell you one thing: I can't imagine going through what a guy like Rex Chapman had to endure. I'd heard all the stories about how Rex couldn't even go home because of all the phone calls he was getting. People calling in the middle of the night, wanting him to come for visits. He'd have to stay over with his friends just to have some peace. I'm sure it was a 24-hour deal for him. That would sure take the fun out of it in a hurry.

I narrowed my list down to Arizona, Missouri, Florida State, Virginia and Duke, although I dropped the Blue Devils when Bobby Hurley committed to them. So, really, there were only four schools that I had to choose from.

Georgia Tech and North Carolina were two other schools that got into the recruiting process extremely late. I was really interested in Georgia Tech because I followed Mark Price and I liked Coach Bobby Cremins quite a bit. When I talked to them, they were straight up front with me, saying they thought they had a great shot at getting Kenny Anderson, which they eventually did. North Carolina, at the time, felt like they had him too. Because of that, I never really considered those two schools very seriously, although they were always in the back of my mind.

I had made an unofficial visit to Arizona during my junior year so I was already fairly familiar with that program. I went there two days before they left for the Final Four to watch them practice. While I was there, I had the chance to meet Coach Lute Olson. That was real exciting. However, while I was considering them, they signed a transfer point guard, so I marked them off the list.

Naturally, the question everyone asked me at the time was, how did I feel about not being recruited by the University of Kentucky? Most of those who asked seemed to assume that since I was a Kentucky kid who grew up following the Wildcats, I was upset or angry because UK wasn't showing any interest in me.

What happened was, after I made my visits to Arizona, Florida State, Virginia and Missouri, I realized that there are other great programs out there. Until I saw those programs, I thought Kentucky was it. But I was wrong.

I also knew the situation at Kentucky. Sean Sutton was there, Sean Woods was there and Richie Farmer was going to be there. The opportunity for me to play didn't look too good.

I never had any second thoughts about not playing at Kentucky. I guess that's because I was being recruited by those other schools with such great basketball traditions. I just moved on quickly. I never sat back and waited on Kentucky. I didn't want to do that. They didn't want me, fine. I was going to move on. Even if they had recruited me, I don't know if I would have gone there or not because of the situation.

After scratching off Duke and Arizona, that left Florida State, Missouri and Virginia as my final choices. I truly felt that I couldn't go wrong with any of them. But there were several things I had to consider: The first thing I was looking for basketball-wise was that I wanted to go where I could play right away. I didn't want to go somewhere and then sit on the bench. It wasn't an ego thing, I just wanted to play. Even if I had to go to a Division II school to play, that's what I would have done. I also wanted to go to a school with a lot of tradition, with a lot of fan support, and with a great coach. I wanted to be on a team where I was surrounded by very good players. All of these schools had something to contribute in each of these categories.

Academically, I think every college in America is going to be good. It's basically up to the individual student-athlete as to what kind of education he or she gets. If you want to learn, you can. Simple as that. You just have to be willing to put forth the effort and to make sacrifices. I'm not saying it's a piece of cake, but the education is there for you if you want it. You have to make it a priority, that's all. I knew I was going to succeed in class, regardless of which school I chose.

I really started to narrow things down after I made my visits. After each one, I'd come back home and tell my parents that that's where I wanted to go. I imagine everybody reacts that way. The impression it makes on you, all the nice people you meet, the special way you're treated: it's all very intoxicating. Never, ever, make a decision right after a visit. That's maybe the first piece of advice I'd give any high school athlete who is being recruited by a college. Make your visit, then come home and think about it for a few days. After you've made all your visits, take off a couple of weeks and try to put it all out of your head. Then after you've done that, sit down, weigh the options and try to decide where you'll fit in the best and where you'll be the happiest. It's essential that you look at the overall picture: how much you're going to play, the facilities, the academics, the coach and the players. There is so much involved. The wisest thing to do is take your time and not make quick decisions.

There are countless horror stories related to recruiting. We've all heard them and read about them. The cheating, the money, the promises, everything. But I have to tell you that I experienced none of that. Every coach and every assistant coach was on the up-and-up with me all the way. Nothing illegal ever happened. Everything the coaches did was within the rules. They all showed me a great time, and everybody did the best they could to get me, but everything was definitely legal. That's another way in which having a father who knows and understands the rules was helpful. He wasn't about to let anyone do anything illegal because he knew it could jeopardize my career.

One night I got a call from Rex Chapman. He was calling on Virginia's behalf. The main assistant coach who was recruiting me there was Jeff Jones, who is now the head coach for the Cavaliers. Jeff played for Rex's dad, Wayne, at Apollo High School. Rex was already in the NBA at the time, but he'd been asked by Jeff to give me a call. Rex said he knew what I was going through, and that he wasn't calling to tell me that Virginia was the best place for me. He just wanted to assure me that Jeff Jones was a great guy. That call meant a lot to me because Rex is someone I've always looked up to and admired. Hearing from him at that time was nice.

As things turned out, however, Virginia was the first of my final three choices that I ruled out. I did so because they had a great guard named John Crotty who was going to be there for two more years. He eventually made it to the NBA. I didn't see myself coming in and playing that much, even though the coaches were trying to convince me that we would be playing together. I just couldn't see how. He was, six-feet, and I'm five-nine. He was a true point guard, and I sure wasn't going to play two-guard in the ACC, so I couldn't envision that working out.

That left me with Florida State and Missouri. The number had dwindled from five to two, but that didn't mean things were getting any easier. They weren't. In fact, it was getting down to crunch time, which meant things were just starting to get tough.

Being recruited was fun and interesting for me because of the various personalities of the coaches and the different approaches they took. For instance, when I visited Missouri, I didn't see much of Coach Stewart. I met with him a couple of times, but mostly I was with the players. They took me around, showed me the city, took me out at night, things like that. I had a great time.

It was a completely different situation when I visited Florida State. I was with Coach Kennedy and his assistants all the time. I went out to dinner with them one evening, then got up the next morning and ate breakfast with them. That was fun because they were extremely nice people. I guess it's just philosophy. Coach Stewart has been at it long enough; he just does it his own way, no better or worse than the way Coach Kennedy did things. Coach Kennedy was real energetic and exciting to be around.

Crazy, unexpected things can happen while you're being recruited. Like the time I was visiting Florida State and had the good fortune to meet Burt Reynolds. How often do you expect something like that to happen? How often does a kid from Madisonville, Kentucky, get to spend time with a movie star? Not too often, I'd say.

The Florida State coaches wanted me to meet Bobby Bowden, the great football coach. I guess they wanted him to try to sell me on the idea of attending FSU. I never followed Florida State football that much, so I didn't really know who Bobby Bowden was. Anyway, we go in to see him in this huge office, and there sits Burt Reynolds. He's an alum of Florida State and a former player there. He goes to all their games. So I sat down and talked with him and Coach Bowden for about 15 or 20 minutes, listening to them tell me how great the Florida State sports tradition is. Burt Reynolds couldn't have been nicer. The two things I remember most about him are that he was wearing cowboy boots and that he was much shorter in person that I thought he'd be. But meeting him was one of the highlights of the whole recruiting period.

The best relationships I formed during this time were with the assistant coaches. They were the ones I was in contact with the most. Coach O'Neill at Arizona, Coach Bob Sunvold at Missouri and Coach David Zimroff at Florida State are three of the greatest people I've had the priviledge to be around. One of the toughest things about choosing one college is that you have to say no to people you've come to care about. It's not an easy thing, let me tell you.

Coach O'Neill may be the best recruiter in the world. It's hard to imagine anyone better than him. Some of the things he did were really wild. And also extremely imaginative. I'd get a piece of mail from him every single day. For about two straight months, he'd send me a piece of chewing gum with a note that said, "I'm sticking with you." He would send me posters, pictures of himself with Rambo's face on it, all kinds of crazy stuff. It's really interesting to see some of the things they'll do.

One of the weirdest things that ever happened, and one that really impressed me, was when Coach O'Neill called me during a game. I was sitting at home with my family, watching Arizona play Washington, when all of a sudden the phone rings. My dad answered, then handed the phone to me. It was Coach O'Neill, who I see sitting on the bench holding a phone next to his ear. He said he was thinking about me and that he wanted to give me a call to see how I was doing. That really caught my eye.

Coach Sunvold is another guy that I became very close to. He recruited me for a really long time. I can remember the first time he called me: it was right after I got back from the Nike camp. At the time, I knew most of the schools that were recruiting me, and Missouri wasn't one of them. Then, out of the blue, I got a call from Coach Sunvold, telling me he was an assistant at Missouri. He wanted to know if I'd made any decisions yet. When I told him I hadn't, he asked if it was possible for Missouri to get into the picture and if they could possibly get a home visit. He said he just wanted to get his foot in the door. I knew Missouri had a great basketball tradition, so I told him I was interested. I got really close to him. You won't meet a nicer man in college basketball, or anywhere, for that matter, than Coach Sunvold. He was awfully good to me and I enjoyed my relationship with him.

Even though I'd scheduled a press conference to announce my decision, I still had no idea where I was going! I kept flip-flopping back and forth between Florida State and Missouri. I would tell my parents one thing, go up into my room, think about it for an hour or so, then come down and tell them something different. It was an agonizing and confusing time.

Finally, on the night before the press conference, I knew I had to make a decision. My dad kept reminding me that I didn't have to choose right then, that the press conference could be postponed until I was sure of what I wanted to do. But I didn't want to wait; I wanted to get it all behind me so I could concentrate on my senior season at Madisonville.

I was still racked with uncertainty, I simply didn't know what to do. One minute, Missouri, the next minute, Florida State. This went on for three or four hours. It was getting late; I went up into my room, wrote down the pros and cons of each school and went over them for about an hour. And decided that I wanted to attend Florida State.

I had enjoyed my visit there, enjoyed the coaches and enjoyed the players. The only concern I had about Florida State was that they had a guy named Lorenzo Hands, a freshman who, at that time, was a point guard. The day I watched them practice, he was unbelievable. I knew he was a great player, and I didn't like the idea of coming in knowing that he already had the upper hand on me. That was really my only concern. But the coaches kept telling me that he was more of a two-guard, which he could have been. So once I overcame that hurdle, I said Florida State is the best place for me.

Then something incredible happened, something that turned me into a Tiger rather than a Seminole.

Coach Kennedy's line was busy.

After I informed my parents of my decision, I went up

to my room to call Coach Kennedy and tell him. But his line was busy. If it had not been busy, I probably would have been a Seminole. But when the line was busy, I got off the phone, talked a little more with my parents, then decided Missouri was where I wanted to be. They had great players like Doug Smith and Anthony Peeler, and I wanted to go and play with them. They also had a senior point guard, which meant I could possibly start for three years.

I called Coach Stewart and told him. He was really excited. He congratulated me, told me he knew how difficult it was to make my decision, and that he looked forward to coaching me.

Coach Kennedy wished me the best of luck and told me that if there was ever anything they could do for me, they'd be right there for me. Like I said, it's difficult to say no to people you care about, people who have invested tremendous time, energy and money in you, people who have treated you fairly and honorably. To this day, I still keep in touch with Coach Zimroff. Did I ever tell Coach Kennedy what happened? No, I didn't. I didn't want to do that. But I do think he found out about it when we played them in the NCAA tourney last season. I believe it was written up in one of the newspapers or was on television. I know there was some mention in the media about it.

Crazy, isn't it, how things turn out? After all that worrying and wrestling with what decision to make, all the pros and cons, all the advice, the final outcome hinges on a busy signal.

But you know what? It worked out well for everyone. I had a great year at Missouri, which is where I truly believe I wanted to go all along. And as things turned out, I would be hearing from Coach Kennedy and Florida State again.

CHAPTER SIX

FINAL DRESS REHEARSAL

The summer between the end of high school and the beginning of college is a strange period filled with great anticipation. On the one hand, I couldn't wait to get to college; on the other hand, I was nervous and apprehensive, knowing that I was about to enter into a different life off the court and a far more demanding level of competition on the court.

Because of those competing emotions, time had a way of playing tricks. Sometimes it seemed to be flying by, other times it seemed to drag. It's kind of like the difference between a blowout and a tight game late in the fourth quarter. In the first situation, time races by; in the second, it seems to stand still. One day, I'd think college was sneaking up on me in a hurry; other days, I'd think it would never get here.

Mainly, though, I tried not to worry about it. I stayed busy by playing as much basketball as I possibly could. When I'm on a basketball court I become so focused on what I'm doing that nothing else matters. Things that might otherwise bother me just seem to disappear when I'm out there playing.

Another reason why I didn't worry all that much is because I simply didn't have the time. As a senior, I was fortunate to be invited to play in a couple of all-star games. In addition to those two games, I was chosen to play for the Kentucky All-Stars in the annual two-game summer series against Indiana. All of that kept me pretty busy that summer.

The first of the all-star games I participated in was the Capital Classic. I was on the U.S. team. The two things I remember most about that experience is that we lost to the Capitals 103-101 and that Kenny Anderson was my teammate.

I was excited when I first heard that I was going to be on the same team as Kenny. I think I was probably more relieved than excited. Being his teammate meant I didn't have to play against him. Well, as it turned out, I was wrong. I had to go against him in practice every day for a week. That was some experience. He came in with the reputation as the best point guard in the country. Some were even going so far as to say he was the best point guard to ever come out of high school. I don't know about that, but I can tell you that he was as good as advertised. Kenny Anderson could play.

For whatever reason, though, Kenny didn't have a particularly good game that night. He scored 18 points, but he didn't give a typical Kenny Anderson performance. It was just one of those nights, I guess. We've all had them.

I got off to a shaky start, then went on to play very well. I had 19 points. Kenny was named most valuable player, but after the game, everybody was coming up to me, saying that I should have gotten it and that Kenny only got it because of his reputation. It didn't matter to me one way or the other. I'd played well, which was the important thing. Worrying or fretting about things you have no control over is a waste of time and energy. Plus, I'd gotten to know Kenny very well. He's a good guy, and I was happy for him.

Next up was the Derby Classic in Freedom Hall. I was on the North team. So was my old buddy Lawrence Funderburke. It was good being with him again and seeing him playing and having some fun. We had a great time together that week.

Another teammate of mine in that game was my future roommate at UK — Jeff Brassow. It was the first time I'd ever met him. Little did either of us know then what was waiting down the road.

Jeff, a UK signee, was under much more pressure to put on a good show in that game than the rest of us. UK fans can be tough critics. Sure, they want a future Wildcat to do well, but if the player doesn't have a good game, those fans sometimes have a tendency to write the player off as a bad recruit. It's really unfair to judge any player on the basis of a single performance. That's especially true in all-star games, where the style of play is usually chaotic and uncontrolled. Some players don't have a game that's very well suited to that kind of play.

At halftime, Jeff didn't have many points, so he came up to me and asked if I would get him the ball. He said, "I've got to play at UK. I need to score some points so I can show these people that I can play." Being a soft-hearted guy (!), I naturally took care of him (just like I have for the past two years at UK). He had 16 points. And I think he impressed the Wildcat faithful, something he continued to do throughout his UK career.

I played pretty well that night, hitting several three-pointers and scoring 18 points. Lawrence had 19. I kept getting him the ball so often that everybody started accusing me of doing it in an effort to get him to go to school at Missouri. I just smiled and said, "I'll do whatever it takes." I would have loved playing college ball with Lawrence.

Oh, by the way, we won that game 128-103.

Those games were fun, and although the players wanted to win and to do well individually, nothing was taken very seriously. Nothing was really at stake. That's not the case with the Kentucky-Indiana series. Not by a long shot. Much is at stake in those two games: pride, prestige, bragging rights. A lot is on the line. These two games are as hard-fought and as hotly contested as you're likely to see anywhere.

The first game was in Indianapolis. I remember being unusually nervous prior to that game because even though we had a good team, deep down I didn't know how much of a chance we stood. Not many Kentucky teams had won in Indianapolis before, so I knew the odds were against us. They not only had the home-court advantage, they also had a huge height advantage.

We came out and played tough as nails, beating them 102-98 in overtime. We'd beaten the odds. Allan Houston had a big game, scoring 33 points. He proved why he was Kentucky's Mr. Basketball that year. I also had a big game with 26. I'm most proud of the way I played in crunch time. I hit a three-pointer to tie the game, then six straight free throws in OT. I kept holding onto the ball, hoping the Indiana players would keep fouling me. They did, and I kept making the free throws. What a big win that was for us. And what a relief. We'd spent a whole week going through two-a-days to prepare for the game. We had worked extremely hard. Not many people gave us much of a chance to win in Indianapolis, but we did. It was a very satisfying feeling for all of us.

With the rematch on our floor in Freedom Hall, we were in a position to do something few Kentucky teams have been able to do — sweep the series. We may have had the brooms ready, but Indiana made us put them back in the closet. They got revenge by beating us 96-88. We didn't play very well, but I think Indiana had a lot to do with it. They had the extra incentive of not wanting to be embarrassed by being swept. Allan had 26 to lead us and Mike Allen of Bryan Station had 20. I only scored 13.

That would be my last high school game. I could officially close the book on my prep career. It was hard to believe that it was over, but it was. The curtain had come down on the final dress rehearsal. Next up was the big time, and the big boys of Missouri.

2. DREAM DEFERRED

CHAPTER SEVEN

WELCOME TO COLLEGE BASKETBALL

My year at Missouri was really exciting. I had the good fortune to play for a great coach, Norm Stewart, on a team that was loaded with talented players like Doug Smith, Anthony Peeler and Lee Coward. Being around people like that can't help but make you a better player.

A lot of freshmen-to-be basketball players move to their college town as soon as they graduate from high school. They do so to get acclimated to their new environment and to participate in the pickup games with their future teammates. Because of the many all-star games I was involved in, I wasn't able to move to Columbia until school started. I did go there once, to enroll and to see where I would be living.

At Missouri, the players live in an apartment building on campus. All the players lived there. It was really nice, a lot nicer than the dorms. My roomate was Jeff Warren, a fellow freshman who came from Michigan. Jeff and I shared some great times together.

Everything about college life in those days was exciting and new. That includes my first taste of college basketball, which certainly wasn't what I expected. For starters, we had to lift weights. I'd never seriously lifted weights, yet here I was, lifting every day, trying to get stronger.

What made it even tougher was that we lifted at six every morning. Getting up at six is tough enough; getting up at six to lift weights is a killer. Since we knew we were going to lift and run that early, we would sleep in our clothes. That way, we could snooze for a few extra minutes. After we finished working out, we'd come back and go to bed.

Conditioning at Missouri was a lot different from anything I'd been through. And we didn't actually start conditioning until two weeks before the season began. I have to admit that I wasn't too disappointed about that. Of course, the players would get together every day and play countless pick-up games. At first, I was in awe. Here I was playing with Doug Smith, who I knew was going to be a lottery pick, Anthony Peeler and those other guys. There was just a tremendous amount of talent on that team.

The veterans were really great to me. They helped me adjust very quickly. But they were also quick to let me know that I was the new kid on the block, that this is college, and that it's a lot different than high school. Don't get me wrong, they weren't singling me out or picking on me. They did it to everybody.

Practices were a lot different from the ones we had at Madisonville. As you can imagine, they were infinitely more physical. Adjusting to the tougher, more physical play is probably the biggest challenge for a player going from the high school to the collegiate level.

We would do each thing in segments. We'd spend so much time on one phase, say, defense, then so much time on another phase. Practices were very intense. Before I got to Missouri, I'd been told how stern and tough Coach Stewart was. How much of a motivator he was. Trust me, he wasn't a disappointment. He was quick to let you know if you did something wrong. However, he'd had a serious illness before I got there, which may have slowed him down a little. At least that's what some people said.

The competition in practices was fierce. Everybody was competing for the same spot on the team or to play in the game. In high school, I knew I was going to play whether I had a bad practice or not. But in college, everybody is the same. The guy you are going against is probably as good as you, or better. That was a big difference.

For me personally, the biggest adjustment from the high school game to the college game was adapting to a different role. I averaged 33 points a game in high school, then I go to Missouri, where I was asked to pass the ball rather than look for a shot. Sure, if I was wide open I had the green light to shoot. But that wasn't my primary function. The coaches were quick to let me know that my job was to run the team and to distribute the ball to the other guys. I've always been a pretty good passer, so that was no problem. It was really just a matter of changing my thinking a little.

We opened the season against Evansville in the Maui Classic. We won that game 68-53, but I didn't play particularly well. I hit just one of nine from the field to go along with two free throws for four points.Welcome to college basketball.

We beat Louisville 82-79 in the semifinal game, then faced North Carolina for the championship. They were ranked No. 7 at the time. They had some great players, (when does North Carolina not have great players) but we upset them, 80-73. I only scored five points, but I did hit two free throws down the stretch that helped seal the win.

Winning that tournament was a great way to begin the season. It provided a big lift for the team. And we were all happy for Doug Smith when he was voted the tourney MVP. He really deserved it.

You can imagine how I felt. Just a few months earlier, I was playing against South Hopkins and West Hopkins, and now here I was playing against North Carolina and Louisville. It was hard to believe. And I was getting quite a bit of playing time, probably 26 or 27 minutes a game. That's a lot of minutes for a freshman. Needless to say, I was thrilled and excited. So were the Missouri fans. After we won the Maui Classic, we moved up to No. 6 in the polls. That just fueled their excitement even more. Every home game was sold out, and everywhere we went, people wanted to talk hoops. I never imagined that much excitement for Missouri basketball.

Our play in Hawaii was a preview of things to come. We started out hot and we stayed that way. We beat Illinois, St.Louis and Creighton. I had my first double-figure game — 15 points — in the win over Creighton.

By this time, we'd moved up to No. 3 in the polls. Then we had to go to Barnhill Arena to face No. 2-ranked Arkansas. It was a huge game for both teams. ESPN, wide-spread media coverage, everything.

The game turned out to be a classic. A real war. We did what very few teams have ever been able to do, namely get out of Barnhill with a win. We beat the Hogs 89-88 on a bucket by Nathan Buntin with 13 seconds left.

I got my first two starts when our point guard, Lee Coward, was sidelined with a cracked rib. I scored 20 and 18 in easy wins over Kearney State and Austin Peay. I hated it that Lee was out, and I couldn't wait for him to return, but his injury did provide me with the chance to get plenty of playing time and plenty of valuable experience.

It was about this time that the school publication had a contest to try and pin a nickname on me. For several weeks, they printed a ballot in each edition of the paper with a list of nicknames on it. Readers were supposed to check the nickname they preferred, or make up one of their own, then mail in their ballot. The names on the ballot were Hot Rod, Turbo, Maverick, Scooter, Sparky, Ford Dog and Napoleon. Pretty corny I must admit, but harmless. I don't remember which name won, but I don't think it was one that was on the ballot.

We continued our superb play when conference action rolled around. We beat top-ranked Kansas 95-87. We also won at Iowa State for the first time in five years. I hit a last-second three-pointer to win that game 95-93.

After we beat Kansas, Doug Smith, Anthony Peeler, several other guys and I rented a limo to take us around town just for the fun of it. We'd stop at every party we could find, get out, tell the driver to wait for us, then go to the party. Everybody thought, "Hey, who are these bigshots?" But after you beat Kansas, you can do just about anything you want, especially in Columbia. That was a great night. Anytime you were with Doug Smith and Anthony Peeler, you could expect something crazy to happen. Those two guys were always up to something.

We kept on winning, improving our record to 21-1. We reached No. 1 in the rankings, and held onto the top spot for four weeks before losing to Kansas State.

Our rematch against Kansas was one of the biggest, most-hyped games I've ever played in. They were 24-1 and ranked No. 1; we were 22-2 and ranked No. 2. It was the first time the top and second-ranked teams had played each other in several years. That game was all anybody talked about for a week.

Anthony Peeler had a terrific game (22 points, I think) and we had another win in a big-time hostile environment. Very seldom does Kansas lose in Lawrence, but we managed to beat them 77-71. I hit a couple of free throws with a minute left, putting us up 73-71 and giving us some breathing room.

We vaulted back to the No.1 spot after beating Kansas. It was nice to be on top again, but unfortunately we didn't stay there very long. Our good times were just about over.

Even though we won a lot of big games, and even though we had tremendous talent, we started skidding at the end of the year. That's when you don't want to be skidding — with tournament time around the corner. That's when you want to be playing your best ball, to be on the "uptick" as coaches and TV analysts like to say.

Well, we were anything but on the uptick. We lost at Oklahoma and at Notre Dame to give us a final regular-season record of 26-4. That's not too shabby, especially considering the schedule we'd played. Neither was our 12-2 record in the Big Eight Conference. That was good enough to win the league title and secure us the No. 1 seed in the postseason tournament. In tournament play, we did about as bad as you can do. We opened the Big Eight tourney against Colorado, the No. 8 seed. We'd killed them twice during the regular season, beating them 104-89 and 93-69. There was no way we could lose this game. That's what we thought. So did everyone else. But apparently no one told the guys at Colorado that they weren't supposed to win, because they shocked us 92-88 in overtime.

Something else happened about this time that didn't help matters — the book *Raw Recruits* came out. I know Coach Stewart was getting asked a lot of questions about the book and about the allegations against Missouri (more on this later). I don't think any of that had a direct bearing on the way we were playing, and I think Coach Stewart did a great job of protecting us from outside distractions, but I have to believe that things like that, things players can't control, take their toll, even if you don't recognize it at the time.

On the Sunday the NCAA pairings were announced, we all went over to Coach Stewart's to watch. Despite our poor showing in recent weeks, we were seeded No. 3 and scheduled to face No. 14-seed Northern Iowa in Richmond.

We really didn't know much about Northern Iowa. I think we heard that name and just thought it was an automatic win. We started out like it was going to be easy, jumping on top by 15 or 20 points. We started cruising and the next thing you know, it's a tie game with two seconds left. Then it happened. A guy named Maurice Newby, a reserve who hadn't been in the game at all, hits a half-court shot to beat us 74-71.

I remember how subdued it was in the dressing room

after that game. How subdued Coach Stewart was. Everybody was sort of in shock. I know I was. Nobody knew what to think. There were some pretty down faces in that locker room. There really wasn't much Coach Stewart could say. We'd just played about as bad as any team could play at the end of the season. He told us that we'd had a great year, which we did; other than that, he didn't have much to say.

I couldn't have asked for a better rookie season. I was put in a position to play a lot on a great team with some great players who made it easier for me. I averaged almost seven points per game, and my 96 % from the free throw line was a school record. My 105 assists and 36 steals were freshman records. Those numbers helped land me a spot on the Freshman All-America team. I certainly couldn't have done it without guys like Doug Smith, Anthony Peeler and Lee Coward going out of their way to help me.

The coaches always had confidence in me and were very patient with me. I have nothing but respect for Coach Stewart and his staff. They treated me well from start to finish.

In every way, my year at Missouri was a lot of fun and a great experience. What I didn't know when Maurice Newby hit that improbable shot in Richmond was that he not only ended my freshman season, he also ended my career at Missouri. I didn't realize it at the time, but fate was about to turn my life-long dream into reality, the dream of playing for the Big Blue.

CHAPER EIGHT

HOMEWARD BOUND

The decision to leave Missouri was one of the most difficult decisions I've ever made. Really tough for me and for my family. It would have been easy if I hadn't cared about the people there or if I'd been unhappy. But that wasn't the case. I truly enjoyed my time there, I liked my teammates and coaches, and I got a lot of playing time. Things couldn't have been more ideal.

But the trouble with the NCAA weighed heavily on my mind. There was just so much uncertainty. I'm from Kentucky, so I knew what the situation had been like at UK when all that mess was going on. I'd spoken to some of the guys on the team, and they told me how miserable everybody was. They said it was just hell. Nobody was having much fun.

I didn't want to go through that. I didn't want the fun, or the joy to be taken out of basketball. Still, though, thinking about leaving a place you love and a situation you're familiar with, and actually doing it, are two different things. The unknown is challenging but it's also a little scary.

Before I could do anything, however, I had to play in the Olympic Festival in Minneapolis. I was chosen to play for the South team, and although I wasn't aware of it at the time, being lucky enough to be chosen for those games turned out to be a big blessing for me.

My coach during those games was Dale Brown. My teammates included Shaquille O'Neal, Pat Graham, Darrin Hancock, Thomas Hill, Anfernee Hardaway and Antonio Lang. Quite an array of talent. But it was that way for all four teams. Every one of the teams was loaded.

The question everyone asks is, What was it like playing for Dale Brown? It was a lot of fun. I enjoyed playing for him. He gave me plenty of freedom to shoot the ball and to create open shots for the other players. He was also very lenient with me. He didn't get on me that much, even when I did make a mistake. I have nothing but good feelings for Coach Brown.

My roommate during the Olympic Festival was Pat Graham. I knew him a little from having played against him in the Kentucky-Indiana series, but I didn't know him all that well. While we were there, we became very close. We just hit it off right from the beginning. Pat's a terrific guy.

Damon Bailey was also playing in those games, and since he and Pat were going to be teammates at IU, they hung out together most of the time. I'd say Damon, who was playing on the North team, spent about 90 percent of the time in our room. We'd all trade stories — I'd talk about Missouri, they'd talk about Indiana — but mostly they talked about all the girlfriends they had. Especially Pat. He had to make three or four phone calls to different women every night.

You hear a lot about Indiana basketball, how the players are stuck up. That wasn't the case at all with Pat and Damon. They are great people. And both of them have a high respect for UK basketball. At one time, Pat was very interested in attending UK. He even made an unofficial visit there. But in the end, both Pat and Damon said they couldn't leave Indiana, that there was just too much pressure on them to play for IU.

When we first arrived at Minneapolis, all the players joined their respective teams and we had a series of scrimmages. During the scrimmages, which were actual game-type situations, I didn't score many points. Maybe four or six points a game. I was mainly looking to pass the ball and set up my teammates. But once the games got underway for real, I began to put up some big numbers. I guess the other teams backed off me because they thought I wasn't going to look for my shot. I ended up playing the absolute best basketball I'd ever played in my life up until that time. In fact, it may be the best basketball I've ever played. There's no question that Shaq had a lot to do with that. It's easy to play well when he's your teammate. He draws attention from so many defenders that it really opens things up for his teammates. The chemistry between Shaq and me was excellent. Things just seemed to click between us.

Until you're actually around Shaq, you can't truly appreciate how big and strong he really is. He's a monster. Once, during one of the scrimmages, Shaq went up for a dunk and ripped the rim right off the backboard. He broke the screw that holds the basket to the backboard. Split it right in half. The janitors couldn't believe it. They said it was impossible to do.

Coach Brown and Shaq got along really well. It was obvious that they had a good relationship. It was also obvious that Coach Brown let Shaq do just about anything he wanted to do. I think that was part of the stipulation, since Shaq hadn't initially intended to participate in the games. I feel certain that Shaq only played as a favor to Coach Brown. I'm glad he did, because his presence made me look awfully good.

I played so well during those games that Anfernee Hardaway, who's now in the pros, was my back-up. He also played some at two-guard, but for the most part, I was the point guard. I think he sort of held it against me that I was getting more playing time than he was. But he was just coming in as a freshman, whereas I already had a year of college ball at Missouri. That experience makes a big difference.

I scored 25 points in the first game, a 112-110 win over the West. Shaq had 26. Then I scored 26 in a loss to the North team. After beating the East 136-125 — I had 14 points and 11 assists—we had a rematch against the North in the gold medal game. That turned out to be an incredibly thrilling game, and a big moment for me.

Tensions were really high prior to the game. Everybody was feeling the pressure. Right before we went out onto the court, Shaq and Hardaway got into a big argument. It was pretty heated. Coach Brown had to step in and break it up. I remember thinking, Here we are, going out to play for the gold medal and we're fighting among ourselves.

The North team was led by Jimmy Jackson, Eric Montross and Damon Bailey. It was a tough team. They led most of the way, but during the final few minutes, we were able to battle back and turn it into a see-saw game. And we did it without Shaq, who had fouled out. Mostly, it was me, Pat, Darrin, Anfernee and Thomas Hill.

With about 20 seconds to go, Damon hit a big three that put them in front by one point. Once we got the ball out, I raced as fast as I could down the court, taking the ball straight to the basket. The trouble was, after I went around a couple of defenders, there was Eric Montross in the lane guarding the bucket. I had no other option but to go for a layup against Eric. I was hoping to get fouled, but he was so afraid of fouling me that he didn't even attempt to block the shot. I just layed it in for the winning basket.

I have won countless numbers of trophies in my life, but winning a gold medal is something entirely different. I guess that's because you've won something with a group of guys who have come from all across the United States and you've done it against the very best competition. It's something very special. Not many people are ever fortunate enough to be put in a situation, where they can win a gold medal. Many people have trophies, but not a lot of people have a gold medal.

That Olympic Festival experience did a world of good

for my confidence. I had some confidence after my year at Missouri , I knew I could play at that level , and here I was, more than holding my own against Jimmy Jackson, Eric Montross, Damon Bailey, and other players of that caliber. I now knew beyond any doubts that I belonged.

It was during the Olympic Festival that speculation about what I might do really began. In a strange way, at one of the press conferences after a game, Coach Brown inadvertently helped fuel the fire by saying, straight out of the blue, that if I ever decided to leave Missouri, I was more than welcome at LSU.

When he said that, the reporters started coming up to me and asking if I intended to transfer. Nobody had ever done that before. Nobody had ever asked me about it face to face. When they did, I must admit that it got me to thinking about things in a different, deeper way.

In the back of my mind, I couldn't help but wonder what was going to happen to Missouri. I did know that the situation there wasn't good. Probation was a very real possibility, and the coaches and the administration at Missouri were definitely in conflict.

I wasn't sure whether I wanted to go back or not. I didn't want to be denied the opportunity to compete for an NCAA championship, which probation would have done, but I also didn't want to be seen as bailing out when the going got tough. And if I did transfer, it would mean I'd have to sit out a year. That was another factor that had to be weighed. With all those things to be considered, I simply didn't know which direction to take.

After I returned home from the Olympic Festival, I immediately got a phone call from Coach Stewart. He wanted to know what the deal was with all the things Coach Brown had been saying. Coach Stewart wasn't angry with me at all, but he was really upset with Coach Brown. He even sent Coach Brown a telegram, demanding an explanation. I told Coach Stewart that I thought Coach Brown was just saying those things to compliment the way I'd been playing, that he wasn't serious, and that I didn't think it was a big deal. I don't think that calmed Coach Stewart down very much.

As the weeks went by, the NCAA kept finding more things wrong at Missouri. The violations kept piling up. I sensed that things were going from bad to worse, which only added to my confusion and uncertainty. Severe sanctions were now almost a given and I wasn't sure that I wanted to deal with that. Plus, I had no guarantee that Coach Stewart would even be back.

While I was at a high school tournament in Las Vegas with my father, I had dinner with Coach Sunvold and I expressed to him my feelings. I told him that I was really debating whether to stay or to transfer. He told me that they desperately wanted and needed me at Missouri but that I had to do what I thought was best for me. As always, Coach Sunvold was up front and dead honest with me.

After I left Vegas, I went back home and discussed the matter with my parents. I mulled things over for a day or two, then decided that I definitely wanted to leave Missouri. I flew to Columbia, met with Coach Stewart and told him of my decision. He said he was sorry to see me leave, wished me the best of luck and gave me my release.

Even though leaving Missouri turned out to be one of the best decisions I've ever made, it wasn't an easy one to make. The fans were great to me, the coaches were great to me, and the players were great to me. I still have some very close friends from that experience. From a basketball standpoint, I couldn't have asked for a better situation. I was on the No. 1 team in the country, I had the opportunity to start as a freshman, and I was put into the heat of battle right from the beginning against teams like North Carolina, Kansas and Louisville.

Despite all those positive aspects, I've never once regretted my decision to transfer. I've never looked back. I think I've been very lucky, things have just fallen in place for me. Having said that, let me add that if there hadn't been an investigation at Missouri, I feel sure that I would have stayed there and played my four years. I would have graduated by now. But I had to leave. There was just too much uncertainty at Missouri.

Once I announced my decision to transfer, it didn't take long for the phone to start ringing. Whether I liked it or not, I was back in the middle of a recruiting hassle. As Yogi Berra said, it was deja vu all over again.

Coach Brown was quick to call me. So was Shaq. They both said they wanted me to come down there for a visit. I told them I probably would. North Carolina was another school that called right away. Coach Smith had never taken a transfer before, but he said he'd break his rule for me if I'd go there. That was very flattering to me. He was on vacation at the time, but he said he'd come back to Chapel Hill if I'd make a visit. Phil Ford, a former Tar Heel great, called to tell me that he'd love to see me in a North Carolina uniform.

Virtually all of the schools that had initially recruited me contacted me again. At first, I thought I'd choose one of them. I'd visited those places, I knew the coaches and I was familiar with their situations. It just seemed like the best and easiest thing to do. Then Coach Sendek and Coach Donovan called to tell me that UK was interested. Coach Pitino was on the road recruiting, so I didn't speak with him at the time. That was the first I'd heard from UK. Hearing from the Big Blue certainly got my attention.

Finally, after much thought, I narrowed my choices to LSU, North Carolina and UK. I'd scheduled a visit to North Carolina, and I was in constant contact with LSU. Coach Sendek and Coach Donovan continued to call and express an interest in me. Finally, I got a call from Coach Pitino. He told me that they were recruiting some other guards and that they didn't have time for me to make all these other visits. He said if I visited those other schools, UK was not going to recruit me. He needed a decision from me right then because other guards were scheduled to come in for visits.

Now the ball was in my court. I had to sit down and make a decision: Did I want to go to Chapel Hill and look it over, or did I want to go ahead and commit to UK? There was a lot of pressure. I'd never visited North Carolina before. Should I write them off without at least checking things out? How did I know that I wouldn't fall in love with the place? How could I be certain that it wasn't the best situation for me?

But I also completely understood where Coach Pitino was coming from. He was just doing what was in his, and UK's, best interest. He didn't want to take a chance on losing someone else while he was waiting for me to make a decision. There was no way he was going to let me cause him to come away empty-handed.

While I was pondering what to do, I got a wonderful telegram from Shaq, saying, "Travis, understand this must be a tough time — I am sorry — If you need someone to listen, talk or just be a friend, don't hesitate. Most think we just play ball — not that simple." I can't begin to tell you how much that meant to me.

In the end, I made my decision to attend UK because of Coach Pitino. I really wanted to play for him, I liked his style of play and I also knew that he'd get the absolute best out of me. Of course I wanted to come to UK because I'd always followed them, but the biggest reason of all was Coach Pitino.

My father and I drove to Lexington for a press conference announcing my intention to attend UK and then to meet with the coaches. We held the press conference in the Hyatt Regency in downtown Lexington. While we were there, my mother, who was still at home in Madisonville, got a phone call from Dean Smith. He wanted to know if I was still on for my visit to Chapel Hill. My mom told him I was on my way to Lexington to announce that I was transferring to UK. Coach Smith couldn't believe it. He said, "This is some way to learn about it." After all this time, I finally met Coach Pitino. He said I reminded him of Coach Donovan, that he saw me as that type of player, a leader on the court, someone who could run a team, and, hopefully, get a team to the Final Four. Hearing that really excited me. He also told me he wished he could have recruited me out of high school, but at that time, he wasn't in a situation where he could.

Until then, I was familiar with Coach Pitino only because of what I'd seen his teams do and what I'd heard about him. I can remember his Providence team that made it to the Final Four. All the excitement, all the three-pointers that Coach Donovan made. I'd heard so much about his love for the game, about how he made players better. And the guys I knew who were here at the time, guys like Pel and Deron and Richie, loved playing for him.

The only negative was that I'd be idle for a whole year. I'd done that once before, and I remembered how hard it was on me. I absolutely hated it. I'm a competitor, I want to be in the battle. Being a spectator isn't for me.

But, as Coach Pitino always preaches to us, what you have to do is turn a negative into a positive. That was the only way for me to approach it. My first love is basketball, and here I was coming to the best program in the world. I'd be playing for the best coach in the country. I'd be playing with a bunch of guys who were not only good basketball players, but also good friends as well. How could I be anything but excited? How could I have anything but positive feelings?

And if that weren't enough to make me smile, all I had to do was remember one other thing: I was seeing a life-long dream come true.

3. DREAM COME TRUE

CHAPTER NINE

THE LONGEST WINTER

When I decided to transfer from Missouri to UK, I knew that tough times lay ahead. And I couldn't have been more correct. In fact, it was even tougher than I had imagined. I'd have to say it was the longest winter of my life.

Two things made it especially difficult for me: not being able to compete, and the feeling that I wasn't really a part of the team.   Sure, I was allowed to practice every day, but always with the understanding that when game-time arrived, I would be a spectator. That was like death to me. I love playing in the games, I love preparing, and I love playing against great players from other teams. I wasn't getting to do any of those things, and that was more than frustrating.

About all I could do was play hard every day in practice, try to improve my own skills, and be as good a cheerleader for my teammates as I could be. Practices can be a nightmare for players who are sitting out. That's because you play against the same people every single day. You run the same system time and time again. As a result, my teammates learned my moves so well that I wasn't able to really show what I could do. Wherever I went on the court, whatever move I made, an opponent was there waiting for me. It wasn't easy for me, or much fun.

The second thing that made that winter so difficult is that I didn't feel like the coaches took the time to really get to know me as a person. That was probably more in my head than anywhere else, but it was a real feeling. I think most players in that situation would feel the same way. It's only natural, because you are, in a way, left out. So you tend to get a little paranoid and blame the coaches for neglecting you. I know I sometimes felt that way. But it's not the coaches' fault at all. Their time and energy has to be spent prepearing the team. Their main focus is on winning games. They couldn't worry about me. Deep down, I understood all that. But I'd always received a lot of attention wherever I'd played; being an outsider was a new experience for me. And I don't think I handled the situation — or myself — very well. I can see now that the coaches really did all they could to involve me and make me feel like an important part of the team. Still, it got to me. I just didn't feel important or needed.

The problem was I let my frustration show in practice. I'd get upset if I made a mistake, or if a teammate didn't perform the way I thought he should, and I'd let my temper get the best of me. When I did it made me look bad. And selfish. A lot of times, I'm sure the coaches thought I was angry with one of my teammates, when I was just angry with myself.

Learning to curb my temper was one of the biggest adjustments I've had to make. And it's an adjustment that took time. That's where Coach Pitino really helped me the most. He taught me that mistakes are a part of the game, that you forget about it and make it up the next trip down the court.

Although I knew what he was saying, it still took me some time before his words took hold. The better part of two years, in fact: my redshirt year, when I had to sit out; and my second year, when I was hampered by injuries all season. I was so bad at times that the coaches compared me to Bobby Hurley, which wasn't a nice comparison. During Bobby's first two years at Duke, I'd heard, he was a terror during practices. He became so bad that the Duke coaches put together a splice of him complaining and making faces on the court. Coach Pitino told me that I was behaving the same way and doing the same things. He was right, too. I was. It was just frustration, something that happened because I wasn't playing up to my capabilities. But that's just an excuse, and as Coach Pitino always tells us, excuses are a sign of weakness. Fortunately, my attitude changed. It had to, or I wasn't going to play. Simple as that. Coach Pitino wasn't going to put up with it.

Contrary to the picture I've painted, sitting out isn't all bad. If you look at it from all perspectives, there are more positives than negatives. It gives you the opportunity to adjust socially, to get ahead in the classroom, and, perhaps most important of all, to thoroughly learn Coach Pitino's very complex system.

Coach Pitino puts tremendous demands and pressure on his point guards. They are a reflection of him on the court. They are expected to be the leader. For me, that's great pressure and I enjoy it. Sitting out that season allowed me to learn every aspect of Coach Pitino's system without having to worry about failing in crucial situations. That was a great luxury. Playing every day against Sean Woods was another big plus for me. He also taught me quite a bit. Basically, I couldn't have asked for a better classroom. Coach Pitino, Coach Donovan and Sean... three point guards. If I didn't learn in that environment, then I shouldn't expect to play.

However, without a doubt, the most important thing that happened to me my first year at UK was having John Pelphrey as a roommate in Wildcat Lodge. I think that's the luckiest break I've ever had. All the guys were great to me, and having their support enabled me to get through that difficult first year, but having Pel as a roomie, being with him night and day, was a genuine blessing.

John was the heart and soul of that basketball team.

Don't ever think otherwise. He was the leader. He kept everybody loose and involved. If there was a team meeting, he made sure everybody showed up on time. He was also a great jokester who never took things too seriously. Except basketball and academics. Those two things, he took very seriously.

John and I have many things in common, the most important of which is a deep love of basketball. That's the main reason why we got along so well. We also knew that we weren't the most naturally gifted athletes in the world, and that we had to do other things in order to be successful. We would always study tapes of other teams, or watch them play on ESPN. We'd keep up with the other SEC teams, with their players. It wasn't unusual for us to watch tapes until two or three in the morning.

Anyone who knows anything at all about basketball can't help but appreciate John. He's without question one of the smartest basketball players I've ever seen. There was nothing he didn't know about the game. But what made John so successful was his ability to read what an opponent or a teammate was going to do. John didn't have to wait until it happened; he anticipated and reacted before it happened.

I think intelligence separates the great player from the average player. That's especially true if you don't have a lot of talent, or if you're not the fastest, quickest guy on the court. One thing my father always taught me is to play hard and play smart. Being my size, if I couldn't outthink an opponent, then there was no way I could play at the major college level. Thinking on the court cuts down on turnovers, helps with shot selection, makes you a better defensive player, everything. Some players can get by on their athleticism, but I wasn't one of them. I've gotten by because I understand basketball.

Although my first year at UK wasn't totally satisfying for me, it was certainly an eye-opening experience that taught me how UK players are treated by the fans. I knew something about the adulation they received, but until you're actually there, you can't begin to appeciate it. Joe B. Hall once said that

UK players are treated like rock stars. I think that's a perfect analogy. We can't go out without someone wanting an autograph or wanting to shake our hand. It's really strange. Everybody acts like they've known you all their life, like you're their son or cousin. I never had a problem with that because I think it's nice that people relate to you and care so much about you whether you or lose. However, I'd be lying if I didn't say that there are times when I'd rather be left alone. It's tough going out with Kim or with my family and not being able to just have a quiet time together.

Wildcat Lodge is our retreat, the one place where the players can really be themselves. You can't get into the Lodge unless you live there or are a friend of someone who does. It's the place where we can actually be normal college students. We can watch movies, play pool, order a pizza, or just sit around and talk if we want to. Wildcat Lodge is the place that keeps us sane.

Don't get me wrong, I'm not complaining about the UK fans. They mean as much to the UK program as anything. I know as a player, I appreciate the fans for many reasons: they travel with us, which makes road games easier for us, and they stand by us regardless of the outcome. Losing is never easy, but knowing that the fans are always going to be supportive makes it a little less painful.

I'll miss those fans, I'm sure of that. I don't know a former UK player who doesn't. Being a Kentucky Wildcat is something truly special, and those of us who have been lucky enough to do it understand how much the team means to the fans. It's not something we take for granted.

CHAPTER TEN

UNFORGETTABLES AND OTHER PICK-UPS

During that first year at UK, whenever I would get down, it was usually my teammates who managed to cheer me up and keep me going. They were the best medicine for whatever it was that bothered me. It's that way for most players. A team is a family, and in times of trouble, families stick together and help each other over the rough spots.

My teammates were the best. I knew many of them before I came to UK, but once I got there, I found out just what terrific guys they were. Pel, Reggie Hanson, Sean Woods, Richie Farmer, Deron Feldhaus and Jeff Brassow were the veterans, and they made life much easier for guys like me, Jamal Mashburn and Gimel Martinez, all of whom were rookies in 1990-91. Those veteran players got us involved right from the start. They went out of their way to make us feel needed, like we were important cogs in the UK machinery. They also told us what to expect once the season began.

It would have been natural for the veterans to ignore

me during those times. After all, I wasn't going to be playing that season. Jamal and Gimel were not only going to play, there was a real possibility that both of them might start. But the veteran players treated me the same way they treated Jamal and Gimel; with them I never felt left out or neglected.

Pre-season pick-up games are another way for the players to get close and to really begin to know each other. Those games are usually played every afternoon from the end of one school year until the first official day of practice in October. The coaches aren't allowed to supervise, or even watch, so the games are loose and wide open. And extremely competitive. Most of the time, there are enough players to have three teams, and if you win, you keep playing, if you lose, you sit. There's a lot of pride involved in those games, a lot of gamesmanship. Players will do just about anything to chalk up a win.

What makes those games so much fun is that you never know who might show up to play. Rex Chapman, Winston Bennett, Kenny Walker, Ed Davender, Sam Bowie and James Blackmon are regulars, and so are Reggie and Jamal, now that they've gone. Those games are great learning experiences. A lot of times, people don't think we work hard during the summer, but we do. And those pick-up games are a tremendous help. They really get us prepared for the season. If you go against guys like Rex and Kenny, you are either going to get better or you're going to be humbled in a hurry. Those guys can play. I've seen Rex come in and play and not miss a shot for three or four games. I've seen him do some unbelievable things. If the current players have some measure of success against guys like that, it really gets our confidence up. Plus, those games are a lot of fun.

Since I've been at UK, I've earned a reputation as a "cheater" during the pick-up games. I won't admit to that, but I will admit that I don't like to lose. Like I said, if you lose, you have to sit out for a game. No one likes doing that. So, if the game is close, the guys on the other team had better watch me, because I'll try to slip in a bucket, or call a foul here and there. The scouting report on me is that I'm not above doctoring the score in my team's favor. It finally got so bad that when I would call out the right score, nobody believed me. But you have to believe me on this, I only called out the wrong score at the end of a close game.

I wasn't the only cheater in those pick-up games. Reggie and Sean have similar reputations, and theirs are as well-deserved as mine. Sean is awful about calling fouls. Every time you go down the court and get close to him, he says you fouled him. Reggie is the same way. The reason we're like that is because we're all so competitive. We hate to lose. No one is really cheating; we're all just looking for whatever edge it takes to get a win.

One of the funniest memories I have from my early days on the team was listening to Richie Farmer and Coach Pitino talk to each other. It was hilarious. They should have taken that act on the road — The Rick and Richie Show. No way it wouldn't have been a success.

I honestly don't believe Coach understood much of what Richie was saying. I'm from Kentucky and I didn't always understand Richie. His eastern Kentucky accent is something else. And, of course, there was Coach Pitino with that New York accent, saying things like "Indianer" and "Rupp Arener." Communication between Coach and Richie was bound to be tough. I can't imagine what those two went through the first year they were together. I've heard stories that when they were talking to each other, they each had to constantly repeat what they said. I think Coach's accent has changed a little since he came to UK, but Richie's is still the same. Together, those two were a riot.

Richie is one of the most naturally funny people I've ever been around. Sometimes he's even funny when he doesn't mean to be. He can keep you laughing for hours, telling all those Clay County stories or about the times he's been hunting. Richie loves to hunt. They tell a great story about the time the team went to Alaska for a tournament, and while they were on the way to the gym, an elk ran alongside the road. Richie made the driver stop the car so he could get out and get a closer look at the elk. Richie also loves guns. One day in Wildcat Lodge, he was coming down the hall carrying a huge UPS package to his room. He was super-excited, which made me curious about what was in the package. I went into his room, and there was Richie with some big rifle he'd ordered, putting it together. There had to be at least 30 pieces to it. I'll never forget that sight, Richie sitting on the side of his bed, a big smile on his face, putting that gun together.

    One of my biggest thrills was meeting Cawood Ledford, the legendary "Voice of the Wildcats." Like all Wildcat fans, I grew up listening to Cawood on the radio. Now, as a UK player, I finally had the chance to meet him and be around him. From day one, he was great to me. He always had a lot of confidence in me, and that's something I really appreciated. When things weren't going good for me, he would always tell me that he had faith in me and that everything was going to be OK. I was disappointed when Cawood retired because I wanted him to call the games when I played my best. He never got to call a game when I was playing the way I'm capable of playing.

    Probably the most interesting person I've met since I've been at UK is Ken "Jersey Red" Ford. Jersey is a real character, and one of Coach Pitino's best friends. Their friendship goes back to the days when Coach was playing at UMass. I remember the first time I ever saw Jersey. It was during one of our practices, which are always closed to the public. I saw this guy sitting there watching, acting like he's supposed to be there, like he belongs. I was positive that one of the managers would ask him to leave, but they didn't. Later, I found out who Jersey was and what his relationship to Coach Pitino is. Everyone loves Jersey because he never backs down from Coach. He just tells Coach how things are. When they're together, they rag each other all the time. And Jersey more

e always had a basketball in my hands. Here I am at age one with a ball I can almost palm.

The smiling shortstop scoops up a grounder. My father has always maintained that I had the potential to be better at baseball than I was at basketball. I don't think I agree with him.

In high school, my job was to score.

Learning to dribble at Dad's sporting goods shop.

At about age two, watching a Second Region game with my father. He was coaching at Webster County at that time.

My freshman year at Missouri was spent with a great coach, Norm Stewart (shown here with his back to the camera).

With Shaquille O'Neal at the U.S. Olympic Festival.

David Coyle

With my good friend Lawrence Funderburke at the Derby Festival All-Star Game.

Winning a gold medal at the Olympic Festival was one of my biggest thrills as a basketball player. That's Indiana's Pat Graham to my right.

Hanging out with the king of hang time himself, Michael Jordan. Later, I took him on one-on-one...in ping pong.

Discussing the action with radio announcer Ralph Hacker after being named Player of the Game.

Chuck Perry

With actor Nick Nolte at the Final Four.

With Dick Vitale after the Vandy win.

*In my senior season I broke Jim Master's UK record for consecutive free throws,
then broke Phil Cox's SEC record before "the streak" ended.*

Getting game instruction from Coach Pitino. Playing for him was one of the best things that could have happened to me. He was intense, he was committed, and he demanded the best from everyone. There's no other way to find out just how good you are.

David Coyle

My fiancee, Kim, waits for me while I sign an autograph in Birmingham. Kim and I will be married in late August, 1994.

David Coyle

Getting a big squeeze from fan favorite Todd Svoboda after defeating LSU in the championship game of the SEC tournament in Rupp Arena.

David Coyle

John Pelphrey gives Coach Pitino a big hug after we won the SEC tournament in Birmingham. During my three years at UK we never lost an SEC tournament game.

than holds his ground. Jersey is another guy who has always had confidence in me. Every time he comes to Lexington, if I'm not playing well, he tells me to hang in there, that things are going to be fine. He's like Coach in that he always stresses the positive. Of course, with Jersey, sometimes I listen, sometimes I let it go out the other ear. One thing you never want to forget about Jersey is that he's a great storyteller. He tells the funniest stories I've ever heard. And like all great storytellers, he sometimes mixes fact and fiction.

When practice for the 1991-92 season began, (the "Unforgettables" season), I was as eager to play basketball as I'd ever been in my life. My exile was finally over. No more practicing, then watching; now, I could practice and contribute.

I was in pretty good shape when practice started. Although there was some rust from sitting out a year, I felt good. My overall game wasn't nearly as off as I'd feared. I had an excellent preseason, playing with poise and confidence. My first public performance came during the Midnight Madness scrimmage, and I played very well. My confidence was growing every day. I felt good about myself and about the team. We all felt that way. I think every player on that team truly believed that if we worked hard and listened to the coaches, it could be a special season.

But just as my confidence was soaring, the bottom dropped out once again— a knee injury that would hamper me all season and keep me from playing anywhere near my potential.

After Midnight Madness, we played a series of scrimmages in Memorial Coliseum. NCAA rules prohibited us from playing around the state, like we'd done in the past, so we played those games in the Coliseum. I was pleased with the way I played. My game was improving every day.

Then, during one of the scrimmages, while driving down the lane, I fell and landed directly on my right kneecap. It hurt pretty bad, but I didn't think it was too serious. At least, I was hoping it wasn't. They took me to the hospital to have it

X-rayed. It was swollen and very painful, but I kept telling myself that I wouldn't be out for more than a week. Then the doctor came in and put the X-ray on the board. The kneecap was cracked right in half. Plain as day. Tears started coming out of my eyes. I didn't say anything, but I remember saying to myself that there's no way I'm going to sit out another season, and that I would do whatever it takes to play.

The doctors told me to sit out for six weeks, that it would take that much time for the injury to heal. They opted not to perform surgery, hoping that it would take care of itself. I never really gave it a chance to heal, which was a mistake on my part. In fact, I not only didn't sit out six weeks, I played in the season opener.

Looking back now, I realize that I handled it all wrong. I should have either gone ahead and had the surgery, or taken off the six weeks like the doctors advised. But I was so anxious to play that I probably lied to the coaches, telling them I was fine when I really wasn't. I guess I wanted to play so badly that I lied to myself as well. It was a definite mistake on my part.

We opened the season at home against West Virginia in the pre-season NIT. At last, after all the waiting and anticipation, after all the travelling and the difficult decision-making, I was a Kentucky Wildcat. I was psyched. In that game I made a pass that people still ask me about. They want to know if it was planned, or if I just did it on instinct. As much as I'd love to say it was planned, I can't. No way I could plan a pass like that. It was pure instinct all the way.

I was coming down the court, and, because of the knee injury, I wasn't going very fast. I knew Deron Feldhaus was behind me, but the defender was staying away from me, so I decided to go ahead and shoot the layup. However, I was going so slow that at the last second, a defender cut right in front of me. I took the ball behind my back, but the defender jumped, keeping me from attempting the shot. So, purely by instinct, I flipped the ball behind me to Deron, who laid it in. It was probably the best pass I ever made.

After beating West Virginia, all we had to do was beat Pittsburgh and we'd be going to New York for the semifinals and finals. Everyone was excited, because the tournament officials had set up the draw so that we would meet Oklahoma State in the semifinal round. In other words, UK versus its old coach, Eddie Sutton.

We were heavily favored to win, but it didn't work out that way. We got killed. Absolutely humiliated. Pittsburgh came into Rupp Arena and simply took us apart in every phase of the game. Talk about having your confidence rocked... that's exactly what happened. All of a sudden, we were thinking that maybe we aren't as good as we thought. To make matters worse, we lost Jeff Brassow for the season when he tore the anterior cruciate ligament in his right knee. But that loss to Pitt was the turning point of that season, even though it was only our second game. Maybe we'd gotten too cocky, or just weren't listening to the coaches, I don't know. But something was wrong. Something was missing. When we lost to Pitt by that much at home, I think we finally understood that we had to do everything right for 40 minutes if we hoped to be a great team or else we could lose to anybody on a given night. That Pitt loss got our attention and turned things around.

We began to win games, but I wasn't making much of a contribution. The more I played, the more pain I experienced in my knee. And the injury really affected my game, especially my shooting. The most important thing to a shooter is his legs. A shooter is like a pitcher in baseball — when his legs go, he's finished. My shot just wasn't there. I only shot 35 percent from the field, which is horrible. I'd never shot so poorly in my life, not even when I was a kid just starting to play basketball. And it was all because of the knee injury.

It was turning into a terribly frustrating year for me. We were winning, but because I wasn't contributing like I wanted to, there were times when I almost felt like I wasn't a part of the team. It was like the year before, when they had a big parade for the team after we'd done so well but couldn't participate in the NCAA Tournament. I was in the parade, but I didn't feel a part of it. Because of the injury, I wasn't physically able to help the team. I'd get my five or six minutes, depending on how things were going. Occasionally, I'd get maybe 20 minutes, but that was a rarity. When I did play, I think I was pretty effective. Because my shooting was off and I wasn't a scoring threat, I tried to do the other things, like making the good pass, playing defense and running the team. But no matter how hard I tried, or how badly I wanted positive things to happen, I just didn't have it.

It got so bad that at times I would lie awake and wonder if transferring from Missouri had been a mistake. That thought definitely went through my mind. I wouldn't be human if it didn't. I would pick up the paper and look to see how Missouri was doing, how Doug Smith and Anthony Peeler were doing. All the guys I played with were still there. I kept thinking, Man, if I hadn't transferred, maybe I wouldn't have gotten hurt. Maybe my career would be going better. At that point, I really didn't know where my career was heading. I didn't know how well I was going to do.

I never could have gotten through those times without strong support from Kim and from my family. Kim was great at keeping me from getting down. She always told me to keep my head up, that better things were going to happen for me. My parents kept reminding me that there is always a light at the end of the tunnel, and that if you're a good person, good things will happen. It may not happen now, but somewhere down the road, it will.

Of course, being around such great, supportive teammates also helped me get through the difficult days. And occasionally, I'd manage to give a performance that made a difference. Like the Florida game at home. We were down at the half, but I had played pretty well, handing out four or five assists. Coach Pitino started me in the second half — the only time I started all season — and I hit a couple of three-pointers that turned the momentum in our favor and triggered what turned out to be a fairly comfortable win. I finished with eight points and eight assists, and was named Player of the Game. I was interviewed on the radio after the game, which I thought was a big deal. I remember thinking that maybe this was the game I needed to get myself going. My knee was killing me at the time, so I decided to just forget about it, play hard and see what happens. But the knee never stopped bothering me. The pain never eased up. As a result, I didn't get to play as much as I would have liked.

I've been asked a thousand times why that team was so successful. Why it was so special. My answer is attitude. They didn't think they could lose. They understood that they weren't the most talented team or the most athletic team, but they also knew that if they played together, played with great intelligence, listened to Coach Pitino and followed his system, they could beat anyone. That was evident in the Duke game. Those players had been through so much together at UK that no type of failure was going to scare them. Nothing that could possibly happen to them could begin to match what they'd endure during their time at UK. So they weren't afraid to fail. They just went out and played the game. And they had such great team chemistry. That was another key reason why they were so successful.

Jamal Mashburn's maturity as a basketball player was essential to our success that season. Mash really stepped up and took his game to a different level and became a terrific all-around player. When Mash first came to UK, he was sort of lazy. You could see that he had great skills — he could handle the pass, pass and shoot — but no one had ever really pushed him to develop those skills to the maximum. Coach Pitino kept telling Mash that the sky was the limit if he'd just improve his work ethic. As a freshman, Mash was just out there to help the team. Scoring, rebounding, whatever it took, Mash was willing. But he never really took over the game like he did as a sophomore and as a junior. His sophomore ear, he was basically unstoppable. Inside, outside, you name it and Mash

did it. Mash was a great silent leader. He never said much...
he led by example. Mash would come to practice every day and
work extremely hard. More than anything else, I think that's
why I looked up to him so much.

Coach Pitino did a tremendous job with that team. He
knew exactly which strings to pull, which players to be tough
on and which players to go easy on. For instance, he was
always tough on John and Sean. But he could get tough with
them because he knew they could take it. Sometimes he'd get
all over John or Sean even though they were playing well. I
think he did that just to make everyone else pay attention.
Coach does that a lot, jumps on a player who's playing well
in order to make the other players realize that they'd better
pick it up and play better.

When we were in Philadelphia practicing on the day
before the Duke game, Coach really got off on John and Junior
Braddy. We had beaten UMass the night before and were going
through our game plan for Duke. Coach was really intense...
really intense. We turn around and John and Junior are laughing about something. They were cutting up, hitting each other,
just having a great time. Coach tore into them like I couldn't
believe. It scared me at first because I didn't know what was
going on. I think it caught everybody off guard. I can assure
you of one thing—John and Junior got serious in a hurry. There
was no more clowning around in that practice.

The Duke game is one of the greatest games I've ever
been involved in. My regret is that I wasn't able to do more to
help us in that game. I did a couple of nice things, but I didn't
help as much as I would have liked.

Although we felt that we could win the game, no one
in the basketball community gave us any chance at all. All the
so-called "experts" wrote us off, saying that Duke had too
much size, too much talent, too much experience, too much of
everything, for us to give them a serious challenge. We didn't
think that way at all. We talked about going to the Final Four,
and we genuinely felt that we had a chance. All it would take

was a perfect game.

As it turned out, both teams played a perfect game. Both teams rose to remarkable heights, putting on incredible displays of courage and excellence. There was no shortage of heroes that night, on either team.

For much of the game, Duke kept a 10- or 12-point lead, and for awhile, he looked as if we weren't going to get any closer. Then, all of a sudden, our press started working. Dale Brown and Sean Woods were having a great game. Sean completely outplayed Bobby Hurley. Pel was also having a solid game until he got into foul trouble and had to sit out. That really hurt. My only real contribution came in the second half when I stripped Bobby Hurley of the ball and we got a bucket. Other than that, I didn't do much more than be a cheerleader. It was an unbelievable game, with the score and the momentum swinging back and forth with each possession. One minute, we'd be up screaming, the next minute, we'd be down. When Sean banked in his shot with 2.1 seconds left to give us a 103-102 lead, we were ecstatic. Just 2.1 seconds stood between us and the Final Four. Just 2.1 seconds until we realized our greatest dream.

But it wasn't to be, thanks to Christian Laettner's turn-around jump shot from the free throw line just as the final buzzer sounded. Like I said, we played a perfect game, so it took perfection to beat us. That night, Laettner made all 10 of his field goal attempts and all 10 of his free throws.

Talk about a somber dressing room. No one said a word for at least 10 minutes. Everyone was just sitting there, crying, trying to come to grips with what had just happened. We were a close-knit group that had overcome great odds to get within a desperation last-second shot of making it to the Final Four, and now it was over. It was difficult, especially for the four seniors, who had gone through so much during their time at UK. We really ached for them.

After a few minutes, Coach Pitino brought out the edition of *Sports Illustrated* that had "Kentucky's Shame" on the cover and held it up. He said, "This is where you were two years ago, look where you are now. Look how far you've come. Don't hang your head. You don't have any reason to hang your head. Be proud of what you've accomplished, both for yourselves and for the University of Kentucky." When we got back to the Warwick Hotel, we were met by hundreds of fans. The place went wild. That's the Kentucky tradition, having great fans who stand by you and try to pick you up when you're down. It was a similar scene at Bluegrass Field in Lexington, hundreds of fans cheering and waving banners. It didn't take away the hurt, but it did make us feel good.

Later, during the awards ceremony, C.M. Newton did a great thing — he retired the four seniors' jerseys. And were they surprised! They had no idea it was going to happen. None of us did. But we all agreed on one thing— they deserved it. All John Pelphrey, Sean Woods, Deron Feldhaus and Richie Farmer did was resurrect the UK basketball program and restore it to its former glory.

As soon as the season was over, we decided that I would have surgery on my knee. Actually, we knew as soon as I hurt it that it would require surgery, but we chose to wait until the end of the year. As I said, that was probably an unwise decision on my part. The doctors told me I could go ahead and play, but for me to expect a great deal of pain. Not wanting to sit out a second straight year, I said OK, I want to play. Nobody really knows how much pain I experienced that season. I never let on that it was hurting as much as it was.

The doctors X-rayed it again and found that the kneecap hadn't healed like they'd hoped. That was because I'd played and hadn't given it a chance to heal. So, our trainer JoAnn Hauser, my father and I flew to New York, where Dr. Norm Scott performed the surgery at the Beth Israel North Hospital. Dr. Scott is the Knicks' team physican, and just about the best surgeon there is. The night before I had surgery, he took us to a Knicks-Bulls game at Madison Square Garden. After the surgery, we stayed in New York for three or four days, then flew back home.

Coach Pitino sat me down and told me what I needed to do if I expected to be a factor next season. The first priority was for me to get into the best shape of my life. He told me that because of the injury, I had gotten out of shape. He said that if I expected to be the starting point guard, I had to lose weight, get in shape and get the right attitude. The weight he set for me was 150 pounds. If I came in at 151, I wouldn't play. If I came in at 150, it was my team. It was a simple proposition. And a fair one. Now it was up to me to do my part, which I did by working harder at conditioning that I'd ever worked before. I spent hours and hours that summer working with Shaun Brown, our strength and conditioning coach. I worked incredibly hard, usually twice a day, and, thanks to Shaun, I got in the best shape of my life. And all the hard work paid off, because the 1992-93 season would be one to remember. For all of us.

CHAPTER ELEVEN

BOURBON STREET BOUND

After the difficult year I'd had in 1991-92, I couldn't wait for the '92-93 season to begin. I wanted the opportunity to prove to the UK fans (and to myself) that I could get the job done as the team's point guard. I knew that unless another piece of bad luck came into play, or something totally unexpected happened, I would get my chance this season.

I'd spent the previous summer really dedicating myself to getting into great condition. I had not other choice, really, because Coach Pitino had laid down the law: either get into shape and get down to 150 pounds or I wouldn't play. I understood why he challenged me to set those goals, and to meet them. With Sean Woods graduated, I would be the only true point guard on the team. Much of the team's success hinged on how well I played. I was going to be called upon to play a lot of minutes, so, if I wasn't in absolutely perfect condition, I wouldn't be physically able to hold up. To not get into great shape, to not polish my skills to the utmost, would have been selfish and irresponsible on my part. Not only would I have been letting myself down, I would have failed my teammates as well.

We all knew that expectations were going to be high in 1992-93. We'd come within an eyelash of making it to the Final Four the previous season, we had several starters returning, and we had a heralded freshman class joining us. Of course, one of the returning starters was Jamal Mashburn, who was, in the eyes of many, the best all-around player in the country. When you have the best player in the entire country on your team, that's going to raise expectations. With all of that going for us, we were ranked fourth in the pre-season AP poll.

The only real concern most people had about the team centered around me. They questioned whether or not I could get the job done. And I fully understood their concerns. Let's face it, I sat out one whole season, and I hadn't accomplished all that much during the year I did play, so they had every right to be worried. None of what I heard or read bothered me. I never got down when people said I was the weak link or that UK should go out and find another point guard. I had confidence in myself, and, even more importantly, Coach Pitino had confidence in me. Ultimately, that's all that mattered.

As long as my knee didn't give me problems, I knew I could handle the point guard responsibilities. When pre-season practice began, my knee was at 100 percent. There was no pain or discomfort at all. Strength-wise, it was also 100 percent. The credit for my rehabilitation goes to Shaun Brown. The tough conditioning regimen he put me through really paid off. We had some terrific pre-season practices. Jamal was better than he had ever been; Gimel Martinez, Dale Brown and Junior Braddy, three proven veterans, were playing well; Jeff Brassow was back and was much improved; and the new guys, Rodney Dent, Rodrick Rhodes, Jared Prickett and Tony Delk, were all making their presence felt in a big way.

I was also playing pretty well, which was easy to do, given the good players surrounding me. My role was to handle the ball, distribute it to the other guys, play sound defense, and take the shot when it presented itself. Of course, the biggest responsibility of the point guard at UK is to be an extension of Coach Pitino on the court. It's up to the point guard to get Coach's message to the other guys and to make sure they follow his orders.

We opened the season with an 81-65 win over Wright State. It was a much more difficult game than the score indicates. They came into our place and gave us all we could handle. Rod had 16 points in his UK debut, and I had 16 points and four assists in my first game as the starting point guard. Despite those numbers, I wasn't entirely pleased with my performances. I committed as many turnovers as I had assists. That's a 1-to-1 ratio, which is terrible. Coach Pitino wants his point guards to have a 2-to-1 ratio or better.

Our next game was against Georgia Tech, a very tough opponent. Much of the pre-game talk centered around the two Travises—Travis Best and me. Who was the better player? Did UK make a mistake by recruiting me rather than him? (Remember, UK ceased recruiting him when I signed to come here.) Who would win this face-to-face showdown? That's all I read or heard for the three or four days leading up to the game. I always find it amusing when people turn a basketball game into a one-on-one matchup because I don't care who the two players are, or how good they might be, a single individual doesn't win a game by himself. It takes a team effort to win, and if there isn't a total team effort, you lose. Even if a player hits a last-second game-winning shot, it took a team effort to get him into that position. The same goes for losing. If a player misses a free throw that could have given his team a win, he can't be blamed for the loss. A team wins together and it loses together.

For that matter, how do you judge two players? What criteria do you use to get an accurate picture? What's fair? Travis Best and I are two different kinds of point guards. He's the kind of point guard who scores a lot of points for his team. That's wasn't necessarily what was expected of me. My role was to distribute the ball and to make everyone else better.

I didn't play particularly well that game (six points, four assists), but my team won 96-87. I would much rather have my stats and a win than to have Travis Best's stats (27 points) in a losing cause. I felt that I ran the team very well, and that, even though I didn't have big offensive numbers like he had, I did lead my team to the victory. And, in my opinion, that's how everything should be judged. Travis Best is a great point guard, but you have to look at how teams, not individuals, do. I've always said that I can make 10 turnovers in a game, but if we win, then I think I've done my job.

We beat Georgia Tech because Jamal and Rod each had 27 points and Jeff came off the bench to score 14. We won because we out-rebounded them 45 to 35 and hit nine three-pointers to their one. We won because our defense was better down the stretch. Hyped individual duels may make for fun reading for the fans, but what separates winning from losing is fundamentals and team play.

After beating, or rather, surviving Eastern Kentucky 82-73, we had to go to Louisville to face the Cardinals on their home court, Freedom Hall. This is always one of the most important games of the year for us, and the one that means the most to Mr. Keightley. He does not like the Cardinals. In fact, making us aware of the importance of beating them is a year-round thing for him. With the possible exception of winning the NCAA championship, beating Louisville is the thing that makes him the happiest. The day before we played Louisville, Keith LeGree, their point guard, came out with some pretty strong statements in the paper, saying, "Yeah, I'm going to dominate Travis Ford. He's not tall enough to handle me and not quick enough to guard me." Most players don't do that kind of thing, but he did. Reading Keith's statements just fired me up even more.

Mr. Keightley didn't have to worry too much about us winning the game. After Louisville jumped on top, we took control and totally dominated them the rest of the way, winning 88-68. We played exceptionally well that night, especially on the defensive end. Mash and Rod combined for 47 points and Gimel had 14. In all, we made 11 three-pointers. But, like I said, defense was the difference. Our press was a big factor, and our half-court defense shut down everything they tried to run. That was a big early-season win for us.

A big thrill for all of us came when we had the chance to go to New York for the ECAC Holiday Festival in Madison Square Garden. Playing in the Garden, the most famous basketball arena in the world, was something we were all looking forward to. Coach Pitino was always telling us how he was born just a few blocks away from the Garden, and how he used to go watch the Knicks play when he was a kid. He later coached the Knicks, so the Garden was a very special place to him. I think he was more excited about the trip than we were. I know he couldn't wait to see how the players who had never been to New York City would react. More than anything, I think Coach was intrigued by how some of the players would handle all the madness you find there.

I'd been to New York several times, so I knew what to expect. I love the place, which makes me different from a great number of Americans, many of whom are quick to tell you that they hate everything about New York. Not me. I enjoy watching all the people, the different characters you see walking around. And there are just so many things to do. I don't care for the traffic jams, but that's about the only thing I don't like about New York.

Along with Coach Pitino and Coach Donovan, going to New York was a homecoming for Jamal, Rod and Andre. They couldn't wait to go up there, but I know they were feeling the added pressure of playing in front of family and friends. That's always a difficult situation for any player, because you want so badly to do well that you tend to do things you shouldn't do. Usually, in those situations, you never play as well as you'd like. That certainly wasn't the case against Rutgers. We came out and just crushed them 89-67. Jamal and Rod had 22 and 15, respectively. They both played very well. So did Andre, although he only had two points.

On the afternoon between the Rutgers game and the championship game against St. John's, we went to the Garden for practice. As we went in, the Knicks were just finishing up. Pat Riley was there. And Patrick Ewing. We got to see all of them. Then, after practice was over, we got to go into their dressing room. That was a big deal for all of us.

After dinner that night, Coach gave us the choice of going to the Knicks' game or going to Radio City Music Hall. Out of the 14 players, only two chose to see the Knicks, and they were Jamal and Andre, two guys who had seen them play a million times. The rest of us chose culture over sports.

Coach gave us a lot of free time while we were in New York. It was important to him that we get a taste of what that place is really like, so he gave us a curfew and told us what time to be back, but it wasn't like he supervised everything we did or was with us everywhere we went.

One night, Rodrick and his brother Reggie said they wanted to take me to some club that was "just a few blocks away." I was all for it, so I said let's go. We started walking, and walking, and we just kept on walking... until we'd been walking for 30 or 40 minutes. Everytime I would ask Rod or Reggie how much farther until we got there, they would say, "It's just around the block." That's true, I guess, but you have to remember, I'm from Madisonville, where the blocks aren't all that long. Rod and Reggie were used to all that walking. I wasn't. We ended up walking a couple of miles, then when we got to the club, it was empty. Rod and Reggie had been telling me what a great place this club was, and how popular it was, yet when we walked in, we were the only ones there.

Later that same night, the team got together and went to the Carnegie Deli, a place that Coach Pitino always talked about. He said he used to go there after the Knicks' games, just hanging out and talking ball with his New York buddies like Larry "The Scout" Pearlstein and Freddie Klein. We ordered these sandwiches, which were huge. After we ate, the Carnegie

Deli people brought out a big cake for Coach Pitino that had "Welcome Back, Rick" written on it. It was a very nice gesture on their part, one I know Coach appreciated.

What I didn't know was that they were also going to bring something out for me. It just so happened that it was my birthday, and once Jersey Red found out about it, he took charge. He disappeared for a few minutes, then came out with one of the cooks, who was carrying a piece of cheesecake with a single candle on it. Naturally, that wasn't enough for Jersey. He had to lead the team in an off-key "Happy Birthday" too.

While we were in New York, Rhonda and Barry Meadows from Paducah came up to me in the lobby of the Helmsley Hotel, where we were staying, and told me that they had named their son after me and that they would someday like for me to meet him. It just so happens that I ran into them again last summer while I was working for someone in Paducah. I ended up spending quite a bit of time with them. It gave me a special feeling to know that someone thought enough of me to name their son after me.

We struggled against St. John's in the championship game, but managed to come away with an 86-77 win. It was one of the most physical games I've even been in. Something like 60 fouls were called, and I promise you that another 60 weren't called. It was brutal. Jamal had a miserable game, hitting just one of 13 shots, but Rod and Gimel rose up and bailed us out. Rod had 23 points and was named the tourney MVP. It turned out to be a magnificent homecoming for him. I only had 10 points and 12 assists in the two games, but apparently the sports writers thought enough of the way I played to vote me onto the all-tourney team.

After the game, a bunch of us decided to go out to a disco that wasn't too far from the hotel. Around 1 a. m. we thought it was time to get back, so we flagged down a cab. As we're riding back to the hotel, the cab driver asked us if we played for Kentucky. When we told him we did, he started getting really angry. He asked us if we knew what the point spread on the game had been. Aminu Timberlake said yes. Then the guys starts in on Chris Harrison for passing up a wide-open layup that would have covered the spread. Jokingly, Aminu told the guy that we meant to mess it up. Now the cab driver is really going crazy, cussing and screaming at us because he had bet on the game and lost. In truth, none of us had a clue what the point spread was. We told him to stop the cab and let us out. It was safer to walk home than to take our chances with that crazy guy.

The Indiana game in Freedom Hall, which we won 81-78, was probably the turning point for me that season. That's the game where I really started to gain confidence in myself. I don't know if it was because I scored so many points (29), or shot so well (10 of 15 from the field overall, seven of 12 three-pointers), or took charge in the final few minutes, but I really felt good about my game at that time. That was just an amazing game. Four players—me, Jamal, Calbert Cheaney and Matt Nover—all had 29 points. You won't see that happen very often in a college game. We showed tremendous courage in that game. We led most of the way, then with six or seven minutes to go, we fell behind. A lot of teams, when they lose the lead, don't have the character it takes to fight back. We could have folded but we didn't. Jamal hit some big shots, and I hit back-to-back threes to put us back on top 77-74. From then on, it was just a matter of hitting our free throws to seal the win.

Another boost to my confidence came when Coach Knight said some positive things about me after the game. Many people don't care for Coach Knight, but I do. I also have a lot of respect for him. He really knows his basketball, and he's one of the greatest coaches ever. So, having someone of that stature saying complimentary things gave me a big lift.

We beat Georgia and Tennessee to give us an 11-0 record overall and a 2-0 record in SEC play. The wins gave us something else as well—the No. 1 national ranking. It was the first time since 1988 that the University of Kentucky held the top spot. I can't tell you how proud we were, knowing that we had taken what Reggie Hanson, Derrick Miller, John Pelphrey, Sean Woods, Richie Farmer and Deron Feldhaus had started and gone one step further. Those guys had laid the ground-work for rebuilding the UK program, and now here we were, reaching the highest level because of what they had done.

As a team, you always strive to be No. 1. Don't ever let anybody tell you otherwise. Even though a lot of people say being No.1 is meaningless, and a lot of coaches and players say they don't need the added pressure of being on top, that's not how we felt. We were happy to be No. 1. Given the schedule we'd played up to that point, we felt we deserved the top spot. We had worked hard to achieve the ranking, and now that we had achieved it, we weren't going to say we didn't want it. Yes, there is extra pressure when you're No. 1. But there's always extra pressure on University of Kentucky teams, so we're used to it. But when you're No. 1 and you walk into an opponent's gym, everybody looks at you a little differently. It's a feeling I like a lot.

Unfortunately, thanks to Vanderbilt, our stay at the top was short lived. We went down to their place and got beat 101-86 in a game in which we were simply outplayed. Forget about us losing because of the pressure of being No.1... that had nothing to do with it. They just whipped us, that's all. We didn't play very well, and we shot poorly from the field (41.3 percent), but the bottom line is, they played better than us.

Coach Pitino was pretty upset with us after the game. He felt that we hadn't played the way we were capable of playing. He was also upset with the free throw situation. Vandy shot 43 free throws and we shot 19. That is a big discrepancy, but I didn't think that much about it because I didn't feel like we had played well enough to win. On the road, you've got to expect things like that to happen. That's why you have to play extra hard and extra smart on the road if you want to win. We hadn't done that. After the loss at Vandy, we lost only two more times during the rest of the regular season — 101-94 at Arkansas and 78-77 at Tennessee. With the exception of those two games, we played with an exceptionally high level of consistency and excellence.

There just aren't many places comparable to Fayetteville, Arkansas. And there aren't many fans anywhere quite like the Razorback faithful. The morning of our game against Arkansas, we went to the gym for an 11 a.m. shoot-around. When we arrived, people were already waiting outside, primed and ready to harass us. Not only did they give us the needle, they tried to come into the gym and watch us. We had to have them kicked out of the place.

As soon as we came out onto the court that night, those fans really lit into us, calling us names and taunting us. I actually enjoy that stuff, because it means they respect you. If they didn't they'd leave you alone. When Coach Pitino came out, their band played "The Godfather" theme. It was pretty funny, but I must admit that Barnhill Arena is a tough place to play, and the big reason is their fans. There may only be 9,000 or so, but they are exceptionally loud and supportive. When they get into the game, they provide the Arkansas players with a great emotional lift.

We felt that for us to win, two things had to happen... we had to play our very best game, and they had to play a notch or two below their very best. If both teams played at their top level, Arkansas, because of the homecourt advantage, would probably win.

We played fairly well, but we made too many turnovers to beat a team like that on the road. Their press got to us somewhat, and that led to them making some spectacular plays. When they did, that fired up their fans even more. In the second half, our press began to cause them some problems, but even though we rattled them, we never could take the lead. Jamal and I each had 20 points, and Jared had 16 points and 13 rebounds, but it wasn't enough. Arkansas had six players in double figures, led by Corliss Williamson's 22.

The Tennessee game... I hate to even think about that one. Talk about a game we shouldn't have lost. That's it. I'm sure every Wildcat fan who saw the game remembers what happened. We'd trailed most of the way, but with Mash having a big night, we were able to come back and take the lead. Then came one of the most bizarre endings I've ever seen. We were leading 77-74 with 4.9 seconds left. At that time, even with Allan Houston at the line to shoot a pair of free throws, I'm thinking to myself that this is going to be one of the really big wins for us all season. Before Allan shot, Coach sent in Jeff Brassow to remind us to block out. Allan hit the first free throw, and because Tennessee was still down by two, he missed the second one on purpose. Because we failed to block out, Jermaine Brown tipped and missed, then Corey Allen got the rebound, hit a miracle shot and drew a foul from Jamal. He went to the line and hit the free throw to give them the win. None of us could believe what had happened. Basically, what it amounted to was a crazy four-point play. We just stood there in shock. There was no way we could lose that game—it wasn't possible—but we had lost. Incredible.

At the time it happened, I didn't realize that Allan had committed a major violation by crossing the free throw line long before his shot hit the rim. I didn't know about it until the next day when we watched the film. It was definitely a violation that should have been called. Still, we shouldn't have put ourselves in a position where something like that could decide the outcome.

Coach Pitino took that loss pretty well. He was disappointed that we didn't do certain things, especially late in the game, but he wasn't nearly as upset or as angry as we thought he'd be. I think that's because he really had a lot of respect for Coach Houston, and thought that maybe the win over us might help him keep his job. Coach Pitino even made the comment that if losing a game like that would help out a good person like Coach Houston, the maybe that was the way it was meant to be.

Really, the players were probably more upset than Coach was. Indiana had lost the night before, which meant that if we beat Tennessee, we would have gone back to No. 1 in the country. But it wasn't to be, thanks to that strange final 4.9 seconds.

We ended the regular season with a 23-3 record, which was better than anyone thought possible. It had been a great, great year. When all the post-season honors started coming out, Jamal's name was everywhere. He was a concensus first-team All-America pick by AP and UPI, SEC Player of the Year, and SEC Athlete of the Year. No one deserved it more than Jamal did.

I also found my name being mentioned quite a bit. The coaches named me first-team All-SEC, while the AP had me on its second team. Being honored made me feel good in a number of ways. It hadn't been that long ago that there were all those questions about whether or not I could do the job. The doubters thought I was the weak link. At the beginning of the year, nobody figured on me doing anything special. It pleased me to be honored, not from an arrogant or selfish standpoint, but because it proved that those who really know basketball, the coaches and sports writers, recognized that I had an outstanding year and that I had been a vital part in our success.

The SEC Tournament was the start of a truly remarkable run that saw us win seven games by an average of just under 31 points. It was mind-boggling. Just winning a post-season game is tough enough, yet here we were blowing teams — excellent teams— right out of the gym. We were so sharp, so in sync, that at times it almost seemed ridiculously easy to us. There were moments when we were killing teams with such ease that it was almost embarrassing. There were a couple of instances where I felt the need to apologize to our opponents for the way we were humiliating them.

Of course, it helped that the SEC tourney was played in Rupp Arena. It also didn't hurt that we began tourney play against Tennessee, a team we wanted to beat pretty badly after what had happened in Knoxville. Going into that game, we had the kind of confidence it takes to go on a roll. We were having so much fun at the time, playing loose and playing together. We jumped on Tennessee 14-0, and quite literally, didn't look back for the next seven games.

We beat Tennessee 101-40, Arkansas 92-81 and LSU 82-65 to win the championship. Against Arkansas, we raced to a 17-0 lead, and when we did, the noise in Rupp Arena was so loud I couldn't hear myself think. To their credit, Arkansas did exactly what Coach Pitino told us they would do—they got right back into the game in just a few minutes. That's typical in college basketball. One team jumps out to a big early lead, and the other team, embarrassed by what's happening, comes right back and makes it close. Even when we were confrotably ahead, we knew it was going to be a dogfight to the end. And that's what it was. It's a good thing we had that lead because Arkansas played great the rest of the way.

I hit six of seven threes against Arkansas and Jamal was the reason why. He came out at the beginning and just tore it up. He was unbelievable. Basically, he got that big lead for us by himself. Because Arkansas had to concentrate so much on stopping him, I was able to get quite a few open shots. It just so happens that I was on one of those shooting streaks where everything you put up seems to go in. For the three tournament games, I made 14 of 22 three-pointers and averaged 18.4 points per game. Even though I played some of the best basketball of my life, I was surprised when I was named MVP of the tournament. Personally, I thought Jamal was more deserving than I was. He was our team.

After the final game, we braved the snow — there was a blizzard that weekend — and went to deSha's to watch the seeding for the NCAA Tournament. We thought we'd be a number two seed and that we'd be sent to Orlando. Coach Pitino had made it known that he preferred Orlando over Nashville, probably because of where the benches are located in Vandy's gym. We thought C.M. Newton had enough pull with the selection committee to get us to Orlando. We were wrong, of course. The selection committee sent us to Nashville, which was fine with us. We were familiar with Vandy's gym, and with Nashville being so close to Kentucky, we knew there would be plenty of Wildcat fans to support us. Although I was confident that we would beat Rider, I was a little nervous going into the game. It's only natural to feel jittery before your first NCAA Tournament game. I suspect every player feels that way. You wouldn't be normal if you didn't.

We did as expected, beating Rider 96-52. It was an uneventful game, but the important thing was that we had gone out and done the job. We played hard, and we didn't take them for granted.

Utah was a different story. Here was a team that was more than capable of beating us. Utah had a great coach in Rick Majerus and a great player in Josh Grant. We knew it would take a good game to beat them. Our defense triggered us in that game... we held them to just 40 percent shooting from the field. We continued our red-hot post-season shooting, hitting 54 percent. The result was an 83-62 win that sent us to Charlotte for a matchup against fifth-seeded Wake Forest.

Everyone predicted a close game, but it turned out to be anything but close. We won 103-69, playing one of the best games I've ever seen a UK team play. Jamal was something special that night. I think the rest of us were just out there watching him. Some of the things he was doing in the first half were incredible. He totally put on a one-man show, scoring all 23 of his points before intermission. At the half, we were ahead 60-26. Don't forget, this is an ACC team we're talking about, a team led by Rodney Rogers, an NBA first round pick.

During the first half, Randolph Childress, one of Wake Forest's best players, came up to me and said, "Stop doing this to us. Call off your press. You're embarrassing us."

I finished with 26 points in that game, but only because Jamal stopped looking for his shot. He could have scored 50 that night if he'd wanted to. After the game, during an interview, I said that now I know how Michael Jordan's teammates feel when they're watching him do his thing. Watching Jordan is something special. Watching Jamal that first half against Wake Forest was special, too.

Now the only obstacle standing between us and the Final Four was Florida State. How ironic. I was going against the school that I almost attended. Situations like that are always a little uncomfortable. I have a very high opinion of Coach Kennedy and Coach Zimroff, and I knew several of the Florida State players fairly well, so it wasn't like I could work up any ill feelings for that game. But because they had recruited me, I also wanted to play well against them.

Florida State was one of the most talented and athletic teams we faced all season. Charlie Ward was a superb point guard; Doug Edwards, Gimel's old high school teammate in Miami, was headed to the NBA; Rodney Dobard was solid; and Bob Sura was one of the most explosive offensive players in the country. In every way, Florida State was dangerous.

You always dream of making it to the Final Four. You also know how hard it is to get there. We were one win away from reaching that goal. Just one win. Florida State was good, but we'd come too far and been through too much to fail now. We were determined that nothing was going to get in our way or keep us from getting to New Orleans.

And nothing did. We handled Florida State from start to finish, winning 106-81. Everybody played well, but Jared was the standout. He had 22 points and 11 rebounds. I had 19 points, Jamal and Dale had 12 each, and Gimel had 10, but the thing I remember most about that game was the three-pointer Todd Svoboda hit in the final few seconds. Todd was a reserve player, our No. 1 cheerleader on the bench, and the fans' absolute favorite player. Seeing him knock down that trey was a thrill for all of us.

During the post-game celebration, Coach asked John Pelphrey and Richie Farmer to come down out of the stands and help us cut down the nets. John and Richie were a part of our success, and having them out there sharing it with us made it all a little more special.

As I took my turn cutting down the nets, I thought back to when I was just a kid and how I used to watch those players when they would cut them down and wave them to the crowd. It's something every player dreams of doing, yet it's something not many ever get the chance to do. Only a select few make it to the Final Four. I was now one of that group. It's a feeling I still can't describe.

When I came out of the Florida State game with about 30 seconds left, Coach Pitino gave me a big hug and told me how proud he was of me. Later, when writers started asking me about my post-season stats, I got to thinking about how much influence Coach Pitino had on my success. During those seven games, I hit 61 percent from the field, 61 percent from three-point range, 90 percent of my free throws, and averaged 16.4 points per game. Those numbers didn't come about by accident, either. Two people were mainly responsible—Coach Pitino and Jamal Mashburn.

During the season, Coach Pitino sat me down, pulled out a stat sheet, and showed me how many three-point shots I was taking compared to two-point shots. I was startled by the difference. It wasn't even close. Coach told me that unless that changed, opponents were going to start defending against the three and that I wouldn't score as many points. If that happened, it would hurt the team. As a result, I began working on a little running one-hand shot in the lane. I worked awfully hard on that shot, and in time, I became pretty good at it. It was the only way I could get a shot in the lane against bigger players. Being a threat to penetrate was invaluable to me because it enabled me to get better three-point opportunities. All of that came about because of Coach Pitino.

As for Jamal, well, all I can say is that someday I'll be able to tell my grandkids that I played with Jamal Mashburn, who will be one of the greats in the NBA when his career is over. Playing with Jamal was not only a treat, it was the luckiest thing that could have happened to me. I fed off of him.

Teams would double- and triple-team him, which that would leave me wide open. Jamal was so unselfish. And so smart. He just knew where I was going to be. We had a great two-man game. I owe Jamal a lot. Many times he gave the ball to me when he could just as easily have taken the shot. He's definitely the best player I've ever played with.

Do I think Jamal made the right decision when he chose to turn pro? Absolutely. No question about it. Only an idiot would think he did the wrong thing. Jamal had no other option, really. He had millions and millions of dollars waiting for him, it was something he'd always wanted to do, and the opportunity was there. Nothing he might have done or learned in another year of college ball was going to improve his situation. And he could have suffered a serious injury if he'd stayed in college. Maybe it would have been him rather than Moon who went down with a torn ACL. Think about how much money that would have cost him. We could have pleaded with him to stick around for one more year, but that would have been a selfish thing to do. We're the biggest Jamal Mashburn fans in the world. We watch him anytime he's on TV, and we watch Sportscenter to see how he did. When the Jamal Mashburn poster came out, we were the first ones to get them. We're just like little kids when it comes to Mash. I only wish we could have won the national championship while Mash was here. That would have been the perfect ending for what was a storybook year for all of us. But the University of Michigan ended our dream.

We went down to New Orleans a day or two before the other three teams. Coach Pitino felt that we'd worked hard all year and that we'd earned the right to go down there and enjoy the Final Four atmosphere, Bourbon Street, the French Quarter —all of it. Our goal was to win the whole thing, and that's what was first and foremost on our mind, but he also wanted us to have some fun. I can tell you that Bourbon Street is unlike anything I'd ever seen before. It was like being at a carnival. We'd all heard a lot of stories about Bourbon Street and the

French Quarter, so we expected it to be a unique place. It turned out to be far more than any of us expected.

You never know who you might run into or see at the Final Four. In the hotel corridor one day, I looked up and there was Nick Nolte. He was there to prepare for his role in Blue Chips, the movie Coach Pitino was also in. I had the chance to meet him and to talk with him for a few minutes. I even had my picture taken with him.

While we were at the University of New Orleans practicing for the Michigan game, I ran into a screen set by Tony Delk, fell and hit my head on the floor. It knocked me out for about 10 seconds. When I regained consciousness, I had no idea what had happened. All I knew was that my neck was sore and I had a headache.

Even though Michigan had the Fab Five and had been to the championship game the year before, we were confident that we could beat them. We had to keep them off the boards and not let them have second and third shots, and we had to take care of the basketball. If we did that, and if we took good shots, we didn't see any reason why we couldn't win the game.

Another key to beating them was to ignore all their trash talk. If you pay any attention to that stuff, you're dead before you start. The Michigan players came out after we were warming up and started screaming and yelling at us. Jalen Rose and Juwan Howard were doing most of the talking. I don't know about the other guys on our team, but for me, all that talk just gets me more pumped up to play.

I think we were a little tight at the beginning of the game. Some people felt that we may have been intimidated somewhat by the Michigan players. I don't know if I agree with that or not, but the fact is, we didn't play well during the first half. About the only one who did play well was Dale Brown. He kept us in the game with his three-point shooting.

Midway through the second half, Dale suffered a shoulder injury that knocked him out of the game. Losing him was a big blow. Up to that point, he'd been our most consistent, most productive player.

We were down by 10 when Mash just took over the game. Michigan couldn't stop him, so we just kept giving him the ball. With Mash practically scoring at will, and with our press finally beginning to take its toll, we were able fight back and send the game into overtime. Even with Dale out with an injury and Jared out with five fouls, I felt good about our chances. As long as we had Jamal, we were OK. We were leading 76-72 when Jamal committed his fifth foul. He went out, and with him went our dream of winning the NCAA championship. All week, the coaches had emphasized the importance of blocking out, and that's the one thing we didn't do well. Failing to do that probably cost us the game. And maybe an NCAA title. I've often wondered how we would have done against North Carolina in the final game if we had beaten Michigan, and each time I do, I have the strong feeling that we would have beaten them. I feel that we would have matched up well against them. They had all those big guys, but we had Moon, a huge guy, and Andre, who was playing well at that time. And I don't think they had anyone who could have stopped Mash. I'm also convinced that our press would have given them a lot of problems. I think it would certainly have been an interesting game to watch.

Losing to Michigan hurt because I really hated to see the four seniors go. I went up to Jamal and told him how much I had enjoyed playing with him. Then there was Dale, my roommate at the time, a player who gave his heart and soul and never expected any credit from anybody. And Junior, a guy who had been through everything, who had gone from being a walk-on to earning a scholarship. And Todd, a terrific guy and a real team leader. It was a great group, and I didn't want to see them leave.

In every way, that was my most satisfying year as a basketball player. Ever. From a personal point of view, I silenced all those people who doubted me, who said the team would die because I wouldn't be able to handle the job of point guard. Team-wise, I knew we were going to be good, but I never dreamed that we'd be 30-4, or go on one of the most incredible runs in NCAA Tournament history, or make it to the Final Four. It was definitely the most memorable and most enjoyable year of my life.

CHAPTER TWELVE

JOURNAL NOTES

Prior to the beginning of this season's practice, my fiancee Kim Garvin suggested that I keep a journal. What follows are a few of my thoughts and observations from Midnight Madness to the Indiana game.

October 29- Midnight Madness is tonight. This means two things: 1) the end of pre-season conditioning, and 2) the beginning of basketball season. People have been in line for Midnight Madness since Tuesday. I am very excited about tonight. This will be my last Midnight Madness. I am looking forward to this season. All day, Wildcat Lodge has been swamped with people trying to get autographs.

I went to Memorial Coliseum around 10 p.m. to get ready for the big night. My back is really bothering me and I need to get treatment. At 11, Coach Pitino came into the locker room to talk to the team. He was in a very good mood. He told us what a great team we could have if we worked hard and played as a team. He told us how we would be divided up for the Midnight Madness scrimmage and the drills we would do.

At midnight each player was introduced to the crowd. I was kind of nervous before my introduction, but as soon as I heard my name, I felt comfortable about everything. My teammates for the scrimmage were Rodrick Rhodes, Jared Prickett, Andre Riddick, Chris Harrison and Mark Pope. We won the 15-minute scrimmage. Everyone got tired real quick because of all the excitement. ESPN kept cutting back and forth between our Midnight Madness, UMass's and North Carolina's. There was a three-point shooting contest between Chris Harrison and me. I won, hitting 15 of 20 shots. After Midnight Madness was finished, I spent some time with Kim and my family.

Oct. 30 — Our first real practice began at noon. Everyone was still draggy from the night before. Practice lasted for three hours, and everything seemed to go smoothly. Jeff Sheppard was the first player Coach Pitino really jumped on. Jeff kept starting the offense by dribbling to one side of the floor. Coach Pitino told him to keep the ball in the middle of the court. Jeff did it again, and Coach yelled at him, saying that if it happened again, he would send Jeff back to Georgia. Practice went by quickly. Coach Pitino was extremely pleased, saying that it was the best first practice any team of his had ever had. My only worry is my back. It's killing me.

Oct. 31 — The first practice of the day started at 10 a.m. It lasted for two hours. I could not buy a shot. My shot was really off. It didn't feel comfortable. The second practice started at 7 p.m. I played much better tonight. Rodrick Rhodes is playing very well. Tonight's practice was much more demanding than the one we had this morning. After practice, half the team was in the training room getting treatment for various injuries. Mostly, everyone was cramping up. Two-a-days take their toll on a body.

Nov. 1 — Day off!

Nov. 2 — Our first practice was at 6 a.m. (This week, we will have two-a-days. Coach Pitino calls it "Dedication Week." Curfew every night is 10 o'clock. It takes us a little longer to get going during the early morning practices. The first practice was OK, except for the high number of turnovers.

The second practice was much better. Rodney Dent is playing great. Coach Pitino jumped on me for the first time when I didn't step in front of Jared Prickett and take a charge. Practice ended with a 20-minute scrimmage. My team won by 10. I played well, except for a couple of stupid turnovers. I need to do a better job of attacking the pressure when being pressed. My back is absolutely killing me! After practice, the doctor gave me some strong medicine to help me rest. Tomorrow will come quickly!

Nov. 4 — Our early practice was very sloppy. There were just too many turnovers. Coach Pitino was a little edgy. Chris Harrison got kicked out of practice for not doing what Coach had told him three times to do. We all played better this afternoon. Even my back isn't hurting me as much.

Nov. 5 — The first practice was this afternoon. That's because this is the first day of Coach Pitino's coaches' clinic. Several hundred coaches came to watch us practice. Several friends from home who were attending the clinic stopped by Wildcat Lodge to see me. One of them was Rod Rhew from Madisonville. Practice was great... our best one yet. Everyone was working hard. Tony Delk was on fire. Tonight's practice began at 10. We just ran through some plays and put in the "Red" press. Coach Pitino is in a great mood because we are working so hard.

Nov. 6 — The morning practice didn't go that well. Coach Pitino went off on the four seniors. Practice wasn't very enthusiastic, and we weren't working hard, so Coach blames the captains (seniors) for not getting everyone ready. After practice, we run until everybody is about sick. Coach is the maddest he's been this year, especially at Jeff Brassow. I called a team meeting after practice to tell everyone to forget about that practice and to just not let it happen again.

The night practice was basically a 30-minute scrimmage. My team won. Everyone is absolutely exhausted. Coach Pitino is in a better mood. After practice, we all got together to watch the Holyfield-Bowe fight.

Nov. 7 —Morning practice went well. It was an easy practice. We mostly just shot a lot of free throws. Tonight's practice marked the end of "Dedication Week." We worked a lot on our half-court motion offense. I didn't shave at all during "Dedication Week." I shaved immediately after practice.

Nov. 9—The first day of individual instructions. Individual is one-on-one practice with a coach. We mostly shoot a lot of threes. Today's practice was going well until I sprained my ankle. It really scared me. I thought it was serious, but now I don't think it is.

Nov. 10 — My ankle is really sore. I sat out individual and regular practice.

Nov. 11 — The ankle is starting to feel better. I went through part of individual instruction. It hurts to jump, but I put up a lot of shots during practice. I was hobbling at the beginning of practice, but as it went on, the ankle got better. Coach Pitino jumped on Andre Riddick for pouting.

Nov. 12—Practice didn't go very well. Coach is really upset with our defense, press and turnovers. Practice ended with us doing a lot of running because Coach didn't think we worked hard.

Nov. 13 — Tonight we had our Blue-White scrimmage that is open to the public. This morning we had a walk-through. We got up a lot of shots, then ran through our offense and our out-of-bounds plays. We ate our pre-game meal at deSha's, then went back to the Lodge to watch the Notre Dame-Florida State football game.

We met in the locker room lounge at 5:15. Everyone, including Coach Pitino, was watching the end of the football game. We were all really getting into it. After the football game was over, Coach gave us our instructions for the scrimmage. We would only run motion offense and none of our out-of-bounds plays, because someone might be there scouting us.

The scrimmage began at 6. The Blue team — me, Tony, Rodrick, Jared, Moon (Rodney Dent) and Walter McCarty

— were trailing the White team by seven at halftime. I was furious at my team because I thought we were playing selfishly. At the half, Coach was pretty upset about the defense, but he totally went crazy about how bad we shot free throws. He told us that we should have been practicing them on our own. The second half was a different story. My team played well, and we ended up winning by 20.

After the game, as I was heading toward the locker room, Coach Pitino told me that a 90-year-old lady in a wheelchair wanted to have her picture taken with me. She said she never misses a Wildcat game on TV or radio, and that this was the first time she'd ever seen a game in person. She told me I was her favorite player and that she had my picture up all over her house.

I played pretty well in the scrimmage. I was satisfied with my performance. I didn't shoot particularly well, but I felt I ran the ball club and got everyone involved. I finished with 10 assists. After the game, my parents, Kim and I went to a very nice restaurant for dinner. It was my parents' 28th anniversary.

Nov. 14—We started the morning practice by watching film of last night's scrimmage. It was not a pretty sight! Coach Pitino was getting madder and madder as the film kept going. He didn't think we played hard or played very good defense. He also said we had far too many turnovers. After about 15 minutes, he turned it off in disgust. This started practice off on a down note. During practice, Coach was in a bad mood because of the film. At one point, he made Tony Delk run the stairs for making a bad pass that Coach called "ridiculous."

Nov. 18 — We had our first practice in Rupp Arena today. These practices are always fun. I guess that's because of the change of scenery and the excitement of Rupp. Practices here are different than the ones in Memorial Coliseum because there are only two baskets in Rupp, which doesn't allow us to break for free throws. We usually practice at Rupp Arena one or two days before a home game. Today we prepared for our first exhibition game.

Nov. 19—We played Athletes In Action tonight. I was anxious to see how we would play against someone other than ourselves. Athletes In Action started out hot against us, hitting quite a few threes. We weren't playing very well, and at the half, Coach Pitino wasn't happy. He thought we took too many bad shots. In the second half, our press took its toll against a tired AIA team. We won, but it wasn't very pretty. Jared played well after starting off poorly. Coach Pitino was still upset about shot selection. He pointed out me, Rodrick and a few others for trying to look for our shots too much.

Nov. 20 — We began by watching film of last night's game. Coach was correct when he said we were playing as individuals and taking bad shots. The coaches put together a splice of the obvious things we did wrong. The film lasted a little over 20 minutes. (Way too long for us to be a good team.) Before Coach Pitino came into the room, Coach Donovan told us he thought there were too many egos in the room and that some of us were worrying too much about scoring. After watching the film, I knew he was right. We went on to have an excellent practice. During practice, I did not shoot because I wanted to break my habit of looking to shoot too much. I think it worked.

Nov. 22 — Coach Pitino came over to the Lodge this morning to interview me for his weekly TV show. We did the piece in my room. It was a lot of fun. I really enjoy being around Coach Pitino in such a loose atmosphere and more of a personal situation. The interview was pretty funny. I made fun of Jeff Brassow (my roommate) quite a bit for not being very neat. Before Coach came, I had to clean my room. I threw everything in the closet. It didn't fool Coach... the closet was the first place he looked.

Today's practice was at Rupp Arena because tomorrow we have another exhibition game. Practice started off badly. Coach Donovan was working with the guards and he didn't think we were working hard enough, so he put us on the line and made us run.   After that, practice went better. We went over some of the things we expected the Australian team to do.

Nov. 23 — We played the Australian National team. They had already defeated UCLA, so we knew they were good. The first 10 minutes was outstanding. In particular, Rodrick was great, making some unbelievable passes. Coach Pitino said the first 10 minutes was the best he had seen any Wildcat team play since he came here. But the Australian team wouldn't go away, even though we were making great plays. They began to go through our press with ease, and ended up beating us. We thought we played hard, but we would later learn that we didn't. I thought I played OK — 17 points, 11 assists, zero turnovers — but as I would later find out, I did not play well. After the game, Coach didn't seem to be very upset. This would not last long.

Nov. 25 — Today is Thanksgiving, which means we have a break from school. That means 20-hour practice rule is not in effect. We can practice as much as we want. We need it. At 8:30 that morning, we had breakfast in the Lodge, then watched film of the game against Australia. We watched about 10 minutes, then Coach got so mad that he turned it off. We looked horrible, and we hadn't played very hard. We practiced from 11 to 1:30. The first two hours were great, the last 30 minutes not so great. Coach got upset, saying that we weren't mentally strong enough to go the other 30 minutes.

From 2 to 2:30, we watched more film of the Australia game. It just got worse and worse and Coach got angrier and angrier. He eventually pulled the tape out of the VCR and threw it against the wall. He told us we didn't play with any heart or with any pride. He was right, too.

From 2:30 to 3:30, we ate Thanksgiving dinner at the Hyatt. No one really felt like eating after the practice we just had. We ate, then went back to the Lodge to get some rest.

We practiced again from 7 to 9:30, and it was much better. Everyone played with a great deal of enthusiasm. Coach was in a better mood after seeing us play like this.

Nov. 27 — Our first game of the season, against in-state rival Louisville, which had some great players like Cliff Rozier and Dwayne Morton. Prior to the game, I was a little on the nervous side, but it didn't last long. The game was being televised on CBS. We played a good first half, although Rozier was really hurting us. We ended up winning by a score of 78-70. Tony Delk played well, scoring 19 points and pulling down 10 rebounds. I had 14 points and six assists. Coach was pleased with our performance, but said that we could have played better. After the game, I went out to dinner with Kim and my family. I'd played 38 minutes; I was really exhausted.

Nov. 29 — Today we started preparing for Tennessee Tech. Tech has a great point guard that we needed to keep under control. Practice went well, which surprised me some-what. I wasn't sure we'd have a good practice after coming off such a big win.

Dec. 1 — We played a tough team in Tennessee Tech. We didn't play well but still won. Coach Pitino was upset with our rebounding. Although we were much bigger than Tech, they competed with us on the boards.

Dec. 2 — We quickly forgot about the Tennessee Tech game because today we had to start preparing for Indiana. We have defeated Indiana for the past two years. Preparing for Indiana is not that difficult... we know that they run a motion offense that features an endless number of killer screens. We worked hard against their motion. This is tough because you have to fight through screen after screen.

Dec. 3 — We met with the media before our 2:30 practice. We always meet with them the day before a game. The media is exceptionally feisty today because of the big game tomorrow. Several members of the media asked me about my friendship with Damon Bailey and Pat Graham. I became good friends with them at the Olympic Festival after my freshman year.

As soon as practice was over, we left for Indianapolis on a bus. We arrived about 8 p.m. and immediately went to

Outback for dinner. Coach Pitino did not come with us, but he did meet with the team a little later at the hotel, which was packed with UK fans.

Dec. 4 — The big game against Indiana in the Hoosier Dome. Indiana was coming off a stunning loss to Butler a week before. They hadn't played since that game, so they had a full week to prepare for us.

We had a shoot-around at 10 a.m. It was freezing in the Hoosier Dome. We shot for about 30 minutes so we could get used to the environment and the goals. Playing in the Hoosier Dome is much different than playing in a normal gym. We then went through Indiana's plays.

During the first half, the lead kept going back and forth. Damon Bailey was having a monster half, mainly because we kept putting him on the foul line. I spent several minutes on the bench because I had three fouls. Near the end of the first half, Indiana made a run that gave them a comfortable lead. Coach was extremely upset with us. He was so mad he kicked over the chalkboard. He told us we weren't playing with any heart or any pride. Again, he was right.

We got back into the game in the second half, with the lead again going back and forth. We kept fouling Bailey, and he kept making his free throws. I was struggling from the field... I couldn't buy a shot. My legs were feeling heavy. I can't ever remember getting really fatigued in a game, no matter how many minutes I played.

This game was an exception. I played practically the entire game, and from having to full-court press and run through screen after screen on defense, I was very tired. And it showed on my shots. We ended up losing an exciting game.

Coach was very upset. He knew we were a better team than Indiana, but he said our shot selection, our lack of motion on offense, our fouling, and our lack of heart and pride caused us to lose the game.

On the trip back to Lexington, none of us were in a very good mood. We stopped in Louisville to eat at the New

Orleans House. When we walked in, a slightly drunken guy was trying his best to make conversation with Coach Pitino. Coach told the man that he wasn't in the mood and to please leave him alone. Coach did it as politely as possible. Everyone went through the buffet, except me. I did not feel like eating. I was hungry, but I didn't feel like I deserved to eat after the performance I'd just given.The drunk guy came back into our room and made a scene. We had to tell him to leave. He said he just wanted to tell Coach Pitino that he was the best coach in America. Coach heard this and said, "The best coach in America? I can't even get my team to run an offense." To say the least, he was still mad.

We arrived back in Lexington really late. Before getting off the bus, Coach got us together and restated his anger. He also told us again that we'd just lost to a team that wasn't as good as we are. He said that at this point, we weren't a very good basketball team, but that the potential was there for us to become one.

4. THE LAST DANCE

CHAPTER THIRTEEN

POPPING THE BIG QUESTION AND FEEDING THE FISH

Since we hadn't proved to ourselves that we were a good team yet, we needed to go to Maui and raise our game to a different level.

Before that, however, I had some very important personal business to take care of. I wanted to ask Kim to marry me. A week or so earlier, I spoke with her parents, David and Charlotte Garvin, and asked them for their permission. They said yes, so they knew it was going to happen. Kim didn't. She was completely surprised when I popped the question.

On the evening before we left for Maui, Kim and I had dinner at The Mansion, a nice restaurant in Lexington. The reason I gave for taking her out that night was to exchange Christmas gifts, since I wouldn't be seeing her while we were in Hawaii. After we ate, I told her that I had ordered a nice gift for her but that it hadn't come in yet. Then I handed her a small ornament made by Hallmark that has a tape recorder on it. It's something new that you can tape messages on. I had taped "Will you marry me?" on the one I gave her. She played it, then said yes, she would marry me.

That was when I gave her the diamond engagement ring. It was very emotional for her. I think she even had a few tears in her eyes. I do know that she didn't expect it at all. We had been going together for four years, and we had talked about getting married someday, but we'd never set a time to get engaged. She knew it was coming, but she didn't think it would come so soon.

Kim and I met just three or four days after I came to UK. At the time, she was rooming with Hannah Miner, a friend of mine from Madisonville. I spent quite a bit of time at their place, and after a while, Kim and I started dating. Things just took off from there.

I can't say enough about Kim and what she has meant to me. She's been through everything with me, the good and the bad. It hasn't been easy on her. Remember, she's had to deal with everything that has happened to me.

Having someone like Kim is important because she helps me keep my feet on the ground. She keeps me from getting too high or too low, too up or too down. You can't put a value on that, especially when you play at the University of Kentucky, where you go through so much, and where, if you play great, everybody loves you, but if you lose a couple of games, everybody gets down on you. Kim never cared if I played great or if I played bad. Not being a big basketball fan, she could care less whether we won or lost. It was good for me to have someone like that around because sometimes I would be down — very down — if we lost or if I had a poor game. She always found a way to lift my spirits. Regardless of what happened, she was always there for me. If I wanted to talk basketball, that was fine with her. If I didn't, that was fine too.

As a basketball player, I've been in my share of pressure-packed situations, but I have to admit that none of those situations can begin to compare with the pressure I felt when I asked Kim to marry me. Believe me, that basketball phrase, "Passing the rock" has an entirely different meaning for me now. I'm just thankful she said yes. I can tell you one thing... it sure made me a happy fellow.

I don't know if proposing marriage is catching or not, but it wasn't long after I proposed to Kim that Gimel asked Missy Diehr to marry him. She said yes, and they are scheduled to get married in July. Missy is a wonderful person who has been good for Gimel. They'll be very happy together.

Maybe Gimel and I just feel that we've gotten so old that our time has run out. I know we both feel like we've been around UK for 20 years. Moon is already married, and Gimel and I will be by the end of the summer. That leaves Brassow, who can't seem to find anybody. No, actually, that's far from the truth. He's probably the smartest one of the bunch. Judging by the number of phone calls Jeff gets, he won't have any problems. So, don't worry about him. He was this year's version of Deron Feldhaus.

The trip to Hawaii turned out to be one of the highlights of the season. We left the mainland unsure of what kind of a team we were; we came back knowing that we could compete with anyone.

It would be impossible to talk about the Hawaii trip without mentioning our bus driver. His name was Joe, and he was some kind of a character. He was a very unique guy who also just happened to be a big Kentucky Wildcat fan. He knew all the players and all of our stats. Although Joe is originally from Hawaii, he went to school in Berea, which explains why he was so familiar with us. When you make a trip like that, sometimes you get to know the bus driver and sometimes you don't. Some of them are friendly and others are just doing their job. This was one of those instances where all of the players developed a close relationship with our driver.

After we first got to the hotel and checked in, Coach Pitino, who had once been an assistant coach in Hawaii and was familiar with Maui, told Joe that several of us wanted to see the island and for him to take us wherever we wanted to go. Eight or nine of us got on the bus and asked Joe to take us some place where the waves were high. He said, "No problem, I know just the place." Well, for the next three hours, he drives us all around the island, stopping every so often, pointing, and saying, "There's some nice waves." Then he'd crank up the bus and we'd take off to some other place. Finally, after about three hours of this, he gets us all excited about a place that has, in his words, "14 or 15-foot waves." He told us how he used to surf on those waves when he was a boy. So, we went to this beach area where our view of the surf was blocked by a big hill. That meant we had to get out of the bus and walk over the hill if we wanted to see these big waves he was bragging about. We did just that, walking over the hill, only to see... a pond. No ocean, no waves whatsoever. Just this small pond. We couldn't believe it. We looked at each other and laughed. None of us knew much about surfing, but we did know that no one had ever surfed at that place.

After that, we told Joe to take us back to the hotel so we could just hang out. I think he was upset with us for a few minutes, but he soon got over it. He was great, taking us around, pointing things out to us, like where Magic Johnson's home was. As the week went by, every player developed a genuine fondness for him.

Anyway, back at the hotel, me, Gimel, Henry Thomas, Chris Harrison, Jeff Sheppard and Shaun Brown, our strength coach, purchased some snorkeling gear and some fish food. We went out into the ocean and fed the fish right out of our hands. Some of the guys even bought an underwater camera so they could take pictures while we were snorkeling. That was a neat experience. It also turned out to be the only time we saw the beach.

The day before our first game in the Maui Classic, we went to an old and very small gym for practice. It wasn't much. The floor was slippery, there wasn't much room, and there were only two goals. During our warm-up drill that we go through before every practice, Rodrick went up for a dunk and shattered the backboard. When he did it, everybody sort of looked around, unsure of what to say or how to act. We wanted to laugh and give Rod some high-fives, but we didn't because we figured Coach Pitino was going to be angry. But he really wasn't. I think the only thing that bothered him was that we only had one goal to practice on.

Our first game in the Maui Classic was against Texas, a club with an outstanding backcourt duo of B.J. Tyler and Terrence Rencher. We won that game 86-61, giving what I think was our best defensive effort of the year. We just did an excellent job of shutting down everything Texas threw at us. On offense, we had a balanced scoring attack with four guys in double figures —Tony (15), Jared (14), Gimel (12) and Moon (11). Jared also had 14 rebounds in what was a huge game for him. It was a solid all-around performance, and the perfect way to open a tournament.

Next up was Ohio State and my good friend Lawrence Funderburke. We didn't play nearly as well as we were capable in this game, but we did manage to come away with a 100-88 victory. Tony and I really shot the lights out against the Buckeyes, combining for 50 points. (I had 27, Tony had 23.) Moon and Rodrick added 13 and 12, respectively.

That win put us in the championship game against an Arizona team that was led by a backcourt tandem that far surpassed the two Texas guards. For my money, Arizona's Khalid Reeves and Damon Stoudamire form the absolute best backcourt in all of college basketball. Those two guys can hurt you in a dozen different ways. They proved just how good they are when they led Arizona to the Final Four this season.

The Arizona game was race-horse basketball at its best. So exciting and fast-paced. It was up and down from start to finish. Without question, it was one of the most thrilling games I've ever been in. Players from both teams kept making big plays. Tony would hit a big three, I'd hit a three, Rod or Jared would grab a rebound and stick it back in. For Arizona, Reeves and Stoudamire proved over and over again just how explosive they are.

Either way, regardless of the outcome, it would have been a great finish. It was one of those games where both teams really deserved to win. In a game like that, neither team is a loser, no matter what the scoreboard says.

Fortunately for us, Jeff Brassow happened to be in the right place at the right time. With only a second left on the clock, he snuck in behind the Arizona defense, grabbed a rebound and put it back in for the game-winning bucket. Final score: UK 93, Arizona 92.

It was typical Jeff Brassow, living by his instincts, coming up big when the game is on the line. He's been doing it ever since he came to UK, so it wasn't a shock to anyone that he did it again in Maui. Jeff is one of those clutch players you can always count on.

After the final horn sounded, everybody was out on the floor, going crazy, celebrating what was a major accomplishment. In the midst of all the madness, I looked up and right there in front of me was Joe, running around, hugging all the players, and giving high-fives like he was a part of the team, which, I guess, he was.

I played very well in Maui, scoring 59 points in three games. I hit 12 three-pointers in 25 attempts, and had 19 assists. The pace of those games had a lot to do with the way I played. I was getting up plenty of good shots, especially on the break, where teams weren't able to match up with me. Seldom during the season did I get as many good looks at the bucket as I did in Hawaii.

We left Maui with a feeling that we had improved greatly as a basketball team. We had accomplished our goal of winning the Maui Classic by beating three extremely tough opponents. Off the court, I think we began to come together as a team. Being away from the friendly Rupp Arena crowds, being in a strange and hostile environment, forced us to forge a team unity that had been missing up to that point. We were better when we returned to Kentucky than when we left. With SEC play coming up, our future was looking extremely bright.

CHAPTER FOURTEEN

THE STREAK

By the time SEC play came around, the thing I kept hearing about the most was my number of consecutive free throws made and how close I was to breaking the UK record of 40 straight set by Jim Master during the 1981-82 season. Believe it or not, until it was brought to my attention, I had no idea that I even had a streak going, much less that I was on the verge of breaking a record.

Everybody was asking me about the pressure I must be feeling and how difficult it must be to deal with. To be perfectly honest, I never thought about it all that much. The only thing on my mind was helping the team win as many games as possible. Individual achievements are great, but they aren't nearly as meaningful or as important as winning games. If I were a tennis player or a pool player, then I would worry about individual accomplishments. But I'm a basketball player, and basketball is a team sport. To be successful in basketball, the individual must be just one link in the chain.

The intensity level really zooms when you get into conference play. That's when things get serious. If you don't do well in league play, you don't get the chance to play for a national championship, which is what it's really all about. Naturally I wanted to do my very best in every phase of the game, including free throw shooting. But I wanted to make the free throws because they would help us win games, not because I was gunning for a place in the record books. Setting a free throw record was the farthest thing from my mind.

Of course, as I closed in on the record, it became the thing everyone wanted to talk about. Was I nervous? Did I think the pressure would get to me? Was I doing anything different at the free throw line? Had I spoken to Jim Master about it? All of a sudden there were countless stories in the paper, describing my standard routine when I shot free throws. Everyone who interviewed me began by asking about the streak. Even the national broadcasters mentioned it. Dick Vitale was quoted as saying that I "played like somebody from the '60s, like a Rick Mount, an Austin Carr or a Calvin Murphy."

It was crazy. I guess when something like that is happening, you tend to dismiss it, or not think about it at all. Maybe that's the best way to handle whatever pressure there might be. But not thinking about it, or dismissing it, is difficult to do when that's all everybody is talking about.

The streak (I later learned) began after I missed a free throw against Florida State in the NCAA Southeast Regional final at Charlotte. It was the second of two, and it rimmed out. I later hit two straight against Florida State, then went four for four in the loss to Michigan in the Final Four. I opened this season by hitting my first 32 attempts, giving me 38 in a row going into the Vandy game. Just two away from tying Jim Master's record and three away from breaking it.

A couple of days before the Vandy game, when interest in the streak was at a fever pitch, I got a good piece of advice from Kyle Macy. Kyle is a member of the UK radio broadcast team, so he's at practice almost every afternoon. One day, Kyle took me aside and told me to forget about the UK record or the SEC record and to take aim on the national Division I record of

64 set by Joe Dykstra of Western Illinois in the early '80s. By doing that, by setting my sights on the national mark, there would be less pressure on me at the moment. And Kyle was right, too. I never gave the UK or SEC records much thought at all.

Kyle also reminded me to just go up to the free throw line, concentrate, and think about the same thing over and over. Repetition, he pointed out, is the key to being good at anything you do. He told not to change anything, and to not worry about what others were saying about the streak or about breaking records. Because Kyle was such a great free throw shooter, and because he was the player I most wanted to be like when I was growing up, his words were a big help and a big inspiration to me. I have always had a great deal of confidence in my ability to make free throws, and without a doubt, Kyle is the reason why. It was because of him that I developed an understanding of the importance of being a good free throw shooter at an early age. That understanding led me to endless hours of free throw practice, and that practice led me to the record books.

I broke Jim Master's record when I made the first of two free throws with 2:41 left in the first half. It was an honor —and a relief—but it wasn't the most important thing. What counted the most was beating Vandy 107-82. It was our first conference game and we'd started off on the right foot. (It was, however, a bittersweet night for all of us. More on that later.)

I ended up going eight for eight against Vandy, giving me 46 straight, which was one shy of Phil Cox's SEC record of 47. I was also within three of tying the SEC single season record of 43. As the Notre Dame game neared, I tried as best I could to put all of that out of my head. All I wanted to do was focus on the game. But it was difficult... my free throw streak was the main topic of conversation among the media and the Big Blue fans. I'm not saying that it didn't cross my mind every now and then. It did. Let's face it, there have been some great free throw shooters in the SEC over the years. To have my name at the top of the list would be quite an accomplishment. So, it's not like I could tune it out completely. I'm human, so I did think about it. But what I tried hard to do was to put it in the back of my mind and focus instead on beating Notre Dame.

With just under eight seconds left in the first half, one of the Notre Dame players fouled me. I stepped to the line and hit the first free throw, tying Phil Cox's record. I also made the second one. Now the SEC record, like the UK record, was mine. Later, in the second half, I hit two more to break the SEC single season record of 43 straight. I guess you could say that my trying to be like Kyle Macy had paid huge dividends.

The streak ended when I missed my first attempt in our loss at Georgia. I knew it was off the moment it left my hand. At the time, it didn't bother me that the streak had ended. It did bother me from the standpoint that we weren't playing too well and that we would need every point we could get if we hoped to win.

What's strange is that I felt far more pressure after I missed than I did while I was closing in on the records. I got a little tense, probably because I was worried that everyone was beginning to believe that I was supposed to hit every free throw I shot. As it turned out, I ended up missing three of four against Georgia.

We got back to Lexington a little after midnight and by 12:30 I was in Memorial Coliseum shooting free throws. I stayed there for about an hour. I was very angry with myself, not because the streak was over, but because I had missed so many free throws. I couldn't remember the last time I'd missed that many free throws in a game. I knew all along that sooner or later the streak was going to end. That was inevitable. But missing three free throws in a single game? That was inexcusable. Plus, we lost the game, which only added to my disappointment.

When you're in the middle of a streak like the one I had going, you don't really have the time to sit back and think about what's happening. That's a luxury you can't afford.

While it's going on, you just go about your business and do what needs to be done. It's only after the streak ends that you're finally able to consider and analyze what you've been through. Even then, I'm not so sure that you really put a finger on it. I'm not sure that you can. Some things happen that seem to defy explanations.

The best I can figure is that sometimes a player gets into a "zone" and plays as if he's on automatic pilot. You hear the phrase "in a zone" most often when a certain player is hitting shots from everywhere, even with one or two defenders in his face. Announcers usually say that player is "unconscious." I've experienced that feeling a few times myself, and it's impossible to explain. You become so confident, so sure that every shot you put up is going in, that you almost become arrogant about it. Sometimes you'll make such an improbable shot that you have to fight to keep from laughing out loud. It doesn't happen often, but when it does, it's an incredible feeling. I think that's the best way I can describe how I felt during my free throw streak. I was loose and confident, and the basket seemed as big as the ocean. It was like that afternoon at practice when I hit 137 straight. When I went to the charity stripe, I had no doubts whatsoever that I would hit the shot. For the first month of the season, when I went to the free throw line, I was "unconscious."

In a way, I was also happy that it was over. Continuing attention to the streak would have eventually become a distraction for me and for my teammates. We didn't need that, not with another challenging SEC race staring us in the face. And especially not after the big guy went down.

CHAPTER FIFTEEN

FALLEN MOON

When SEC play began, we were a pretty confident team. The tourney win in Maui was a turning point for us because it gave us a reason to believe in ourselves. Even though we were still a young team, we felt that we could win the SEC championship. We knew it would be tough, but we had confidence that we could do it.

After opening league play with an impressive win over a talented and experienced Vanderbilt team, we should have been celebrating our good start. Instead, when that game was over, our locker room was like a morgue. There were plenty of tears, and no celebration.

The reason for our gloom was the injury to Moon Dent, who went down in the first half after colliding with Vandy's Bryan Milburn. When it happened, I was on the court with my back turned to the play. When I turned around and saw Moon on the floor grimacing in pain, my first reaction was that he had twisted an ankle. I really didn't think that much about it. Even as they were carrying him off the floor and into the training room, I was telling myself that he would be all right and that he'd probably play in the second half.

Later in the first half, Coach Pitino took me out of the game for a quick breather, and while I was sitting there, someone came up and told Coach that Moon had torn his ACL. Coach Pitino then told Coach Donovan, and that's when I first learned how serious the injury was. I could tell from the tone in Coach's voice that he was really upset. I remember thinking at the time that maybe it wasn't as bad as the doctor first thought. But when I got back into the dressing room at the half and saw Moon lying there on the table, I knew it was bad. I could tell by how much pain he was in. I went over to Moon and told him to hang in there and to keep his head up.

After the game, it really hit me hard. I wasn't concerned about the team — we would compensate somehow—but I was very worried about Moon. I was concerned about what would happen to him. This was his senior year, his last season of college ball. He was having a good enough year that he was likely to be an NBA draft pick. Now that was in doubt.

When everyone else had dressed and gone, I sat alone for a few minutes in the locker room, thinking about how much Moon meant to me, and how much I wanted him to do well. Tears just started coming out of my eyes. I couldn't help wondering how much of a blow this was going to be to him and his life. It was probably going to change things forever.

Moon's absence totally turned things upside down for the team. In many ways, from a strategy standpoint, we had to go back to the drawing board. Think about it. With Moon, we had one of the top centers in the country, a wide-body who could score, rebound and block shots. He could do everything. We were lucky to have Andre, but Andre isn't as complete a player as Moon. Having them both, along with Gimel, meant we had 10 to 15 fouls to give at the center position. Losing Moon put greater pressure on Andre, who, I think, responded to the challenge in a positive way. But Moon's absence hurt, there's just no way around it.

I knew Moon's going down was bound to have a

tremendous affect on me and my game. There was no way it couldn't. Not only did his presence as a scoring threat down low open things up for me on the perimeter, he also came out and set some big-time screens that people guarding me just couldn't get around. I'd come off the screen wide open for the three. Other times I would get the ball to him down low and he would immediately kick it back out to me for the jumper. That was all going to change now that we didn't have his inside power and scoring ability.

Not having Moon put a lot of extra pressure on the coaching staff to come up with ways to offset his loss. One of the first things Coach Pitino did was to stress to us the importance of not falling into a shoot-the-three-only mentality. Coach made an extra effort for us to take the ball inside even more than before. People associate Coach Pitino's teams with the three-point shot, but that approach is only successful if you have a solid inside game. The best way to get a good three-point shot is from inside-out. He didn't want us to forget that now that Moon was no longer playing.

One of the biggest changes was that our inside guys started working on their low-post moves two and three times a day. Sometimes for 30 or 40 minutes, the guards would do nothing but pass to the big guys down on the block so they could work on their moves. For us to overcome Moon's injury, improvement by our inside people was essential. Without question, the player who was under the gun the most was Walter McCarty. He had to take his game to a different level if we had any hope of having a successful season. And I think he did just that.

After losing at Georgia, we bounced back to beat Ole Miss in Freedom Hall and Tennessee in Rupp Arena. Walter had one of his best games of the year against Ole Miss, scoring 24 points, including hitting four of five three-point attempts. Walter is an enormously talented player who got off to a slow start because he'd had to sit out all of last season. As the season went on, and as he gained more confidence and more experience, he developed into a good player. The only thing standing between Walter and greatness is lack of strength. If he picks up a few pounds and gets a little stronger, he'll be something special.

With an SEC record of 3-1, we went to Gainesville to face Florida. Florida, under Lon Kruger, was playing very well at the time. But so were we. I don't think any of us thought for a second that we would lose the game. What we ran into in Gainesville was one of the most hostile crowds I've ever played in front of. The place was sold out, and the fans were on us from the second we walked out onto the court until the game was over.

We lost 59-57 in what was a terrible performance. Embarrassing, almost. We didn't do many things right in that game, especially during the final few minutes. I'm not taking anything away from Florida, but we stunk up the place. We got caught up in taking too many questionable shots. When Florida got ahead, I think we tried to catch up all at once, which you can't do. As a result, we took too many bad shots and made too many poor decisions to beat a team as good as Florida. I can assure you that Coach Pitino wasn't very pleased with us after that loss.

Right on the heels of that game was a trip to Starkville for a game against a dangerous Mississippi State team that was having its best season in years. If we went down there and played like we did in Gainesville, a second straight loss was a certainty. Losing back-to-back games is something that Coach Pitino can't tolerate, and if you go back and check the record since he's been at UK, with the exception of his first year there, it hasn't happened very often. I think we're all too scared of him to lose two in a row.

We played very well in Starkville, winning rather easily by a score of 86-70. I had 17 points, but for the second time this season, I missed three free throws in a game. As you can imagine, I wasn't too pleased about that. I only missed 10 free throws the entire season, and six of those came against Georgia and Mississippi State. For the year, I made 103 of 113 for 91.2 percent. Take away the Georgia and Mississippi State games and I would have had a magnificent year at the free throw stripe.

After the Mississippi State game, we came back with two

totally different performances — a lousy one against South Carolina and a terrific one against Auburn.

Thanks to a big 25-point effort from Jeff Brassow and a 10-point, 17-rebound effort from Jared Prickett, we were able to pull away in the second half to beat South Carolina 79-67 in Rupp Arena. It was just one of those games where we never really got untracked. Had we been playing away from home, or had Jeff and Jared not picked us up, we probably would have lost. South Carolina outplayed us, but we did just enough good things at the right time to sneak away with a win.

Auburn was another story entirely. At the time, the Tigers were at the bottom of the SEC standings, which was difficult to figure since they had two first-team All-SEC players in Wesley Person and Aaron Swinson. What we had to do was to keep in mind that this was a team with enough talent to beat any team in the country on a given night.

Tony had a great game at Auburn, finishing with 25 points and seven rebounds. Rod had 19 points, while Andre had 16. Their play was instrumental in helping us come away with a 91-74 win.

It's a good thing that those guys stepped up and played well in the wins over South Carolina and Auburn because I sure didn't do much to help out. I had three points against the Gamecocks and eight against Auburn. In those two games, I made just three of 11 field goal attempts. The only good thing I can say about my performance is that I did contribute 11 assists.

I couldn't get down on myself. None of us could. We had to stay positive at this stage of the season, because coming up was a seven-game stretch that would test us in every way, both physically and mentally.

CHAPTER SIXTEEN

DEADLY STRETCH, AMAZING COMEBACK

Alabama at home, UMass in the Meadowlands, Arkansas at home, then Syracuse, LSU, Vanderbilt and Tennessee on the road... whoever was responsible for putting that schedule together obviously wanted to find out how much character we had. That's a brutal stretch of games, no matter how you look at it. And it would, indeed, test us. By the time that stretch was over, we had gone through our highest and lowest moments of the entire season.

To everyone's surprise, the Alabama game turned out to be a laugher. We won 82-57. None of us expected to beat them that convincingly. Alabama always has excellent size and quickness, and they always get after you pretty good on defense and on the boards. But on this night, we handled them with no problems. Rod had 23 and Tony had 21 to lead us.

Of course, our game with UMass had a lot of hype because of the close friendship between Coach Pitino and Coach John Calipari. To us, the added hype meant very little.

All we saw was a very tough opponent, a team we wanted to beat because it would mean a good start to the deadly stretch we were beginning. Beyond that, nothing else mattered.

We went up to the New York area a couple of days before the game so we could get in some prectices in the Meadowlands. One day after we'd finished practicing, the San Antonio Spurs came in and had a walk-through. We stayed and watch, amazed by the things David Robinson and Dennis Rodman were doing. I had the chance to see Chris Whitney, a good friend of mine who played at Hopkinsville and who is now a member of the Spurs. We spoke for a few minutes before he had to practice and we had to leave. It was nice seeing him again and talking about old times. After practice, we went out to eat at a great restaurant in New York City. To no one's surprise, it was an Italian restaurant.

In some ways, our game against UMass was the most different game we played all season. It was such a slow-down game. I think Coach was content to let that happen because it was the kind of game you often get into once the NCAA tournament begins. I think he wanted to see how we would respond to a slower tempo.

It was nip and tuck from beginning to end, with neither team able to establish a clear-cut advantage. Even when we got behind, we didn't abandon our game plan. Inside the last couple of minutes, we really played an intelligent, thoughtful game. We executed on both ends of the court, we hit our free throws, and we took nothing but good shots. After being down for much of the game, we fought back to take a 67-64 lead with just a few seconds remaining. UMass had the ball out on the sideline, and when Coach Calipari saw our defensive alignment, he immediately called a time out. We went back to the huddle and Coach Pitino told us that we weren't going to change anything, that we would play a zone, with a heavy emphasis on defending against the three-point shot. UMass got the ball inbounds to a player near me. He took a couple of dribbles, then went up for a three-point attempt. Luckily, I was able to get to him and challenge the shot, which was off the mark. We escaped with the 67-64 win.

Tony hit a couple of key shots for us down the stretch to help us gain control of the game. Jared also stood out, scoring 17 points and pulling down 15 rebounds.

It was a relief to get UMass behind us and safely into the win column because next up was Arkansas and its "40 minutes of hell" brand of basketball. One thing we knew for sure... this wasn't going to be a slow-tempo game. Not by a longshot. This one would be running and shooting, trapping and pressing for all 94-feet.

I think it's safe to say that there is no lack of confidence among the Arkansas players. No matter who they play, or where, those guys go in thinking they are going to win. They have an arrogance about them, but most of the time they back it up by beating people on the court, where it really counts. They don't just talk the talk like a lot of teams do.

The last time we lost in Rupp Arena was during the "Unforgettables" season. The team that beat us? Arkansas. They came into our place and kicked us pretty good, winning by a score of 105-88. Losing at home is one of the worst feelings in the world. Losing at home to a cocky team like Arkansas is an even worse feeling. It practically makes you sick. When they beat us in Rupp Arena, their players were waving to our fans, holding up one finger signifying that "We're No. 1." It really gets to you, having to sit there and take it. You feel like you've let the UK fans down in a big way.

I have a lot of respect for Nolan Richardson and the Arkansas players. They play an exciting brand of basketball, a style that closely mirrors the style we play. They really attack on offense, and they are relentless on defense. And, like Coach Pitino's teams, they won't succumb to hostile environments.

But those Razorback fans... now that's another story. Talk about getting after people. Those folks wrote the book on it. And, boy, are they arrogant! They don't think any team exists other than their beloved Razorbacks. It's remarkable how Arkansas came into the SEC and right from the beginning, became such big rivals with Kentucky. They may have been the new kids on the block, but it didn't take them long to gain respect. I guess a rivalry between UK and Arkansas was inevitable, given the fact that they have two of the six or seven best basketball programs in the country.

In preparing for Arkansas, Coach Pitino told us that two things were critical if we wanted to be successful — we had to handle their pressure, and we had to prevent them from getting easy buckets on run-outs. He emphasized a thousand times how Arkansas loved to release a player early for a run-out, and how important it was for us to rotate properly on defense so that one or two of us would be back to stop it. He also told us that because Arkansas likes to release early, they are vulnerable on the boards, and that if we did a solid rebounding job, we would get some second and third shots. Mainly, Coach told us that as good as Arkansas is, they almost always give you a chance to beat them.

In my opinion, our first half performance against Arkansas may have been the best 20 minutes of basketball we played all year. We were making the extra pass, we were taking great shots, we were handling their pressure, and we stopped their run-outs.We were up 47-41 and feeling very confident. But things turned around in the second half. We turned the ball over too many times, and we let them get some breakaway dunks that really got them pumped up.

Once that happened, once they got some confidence, things just started to snowball. We couldn't hang with them. Scott Thurman killed us from the outside and Corliss Williamson was more than we could handle down in the paint. They ended up beating us 90-82.

At that point in the season, Arkansas was better than us. I don't think there's any question about it. Still, we should have won that game. The reason we didn't win is because we didn't play with the same degree of intensity in the second half that we had in the first half. When Arkansas took their game to a different level, we failed to rise up and meet the challenge.

Coach Pitino was disappointed in our lack of mental toughness in that game. He felt that once Arkansas took the lead in the final minutes, we caved in and gave up. He said if that had happened to his past UK teams, they would have fought back. Losing the lead wouldn't have bothered them.

I think Coach was right, too. We didn't fight back as hard as we should have. And I can't put my finger on why we didn't. Maybe we had battled so long and so hard in that game that we were so mentally tired that we didn't have anything left to give. Or maybe our maturity level and lack of experience showed. I'm not knocking Arkansas at all — they whipped us — but no team should ever come into Rupp Arena and beat us.

Now we were really under the gun. Next up was a trip to Syracuse, where we had to face the Orangemen on national TV in front of 32,000 fans in the Carrier Dome. That's not exactly the situation you want when you're trying to bounce back from a tough and emotional loss.

It seems that we keep running into teams with prime-time backcourt players. Arizona, Texas, Vanderbilt, Louisville, Florida... those teams didn't have just one outstanding guard. They had two. Syracuse certainly belongs in that group. Adrian Autry and Lawrence Moten are terrific basketball players who can do so many things to hurt you. We knew that if we wanted to beat Syracuse, we had to stop their guards.

I had played with Adrian and Lawrence the previous summer during tryouts for the World University Games, so I was very familiar with them. I didn't need a scouting report to tell me that those two guys can play. I had seen what they could do up-close and personal.

Despite the difficulty of playing in the Carrier Dome, we all thought this was a road game we definitely could win. We didn't play all that badly, either. It was just that Syracuse played a great game. Autry was on fire...he kept knocking down one difficult shot after another. Tony and Rod had 27 and 18 points for us, but it wasn't enough. Syracuse won 93-85.

It was a game in which we never got going like we should have, never hit that one big spurt that we usually have. It was also the first time in two years that we had lost back-to-back games.

I was terribly disappointed in the way I played against Syracuse. Forget the poor shooting or the low point total. My disappointment stemmed from not being the leader I should have been. I didn't pull the guys together and make them play, make them get their stuff together, and tell them that we've got to win this game. I didn't respond the way a senior point guard should have. Because of that, I was very, very down after the game.

We had an informal team meeting in the locker room after the Syracuse game, one of those little heart-to-heart chats where you say what's on your mind and get a few things off your chest. There was no anger or animosity, no finger point-ing at all, just a lot of discussion among the players. We just stood up and mentioned some things that we thought were obviously wrong.

One of the areas that we addressed was the need for certain individuals to step up and start taking a bigger role. Some of the guys were content to stay in the background. That couldn't continue if we were going to be successful. Those players whose personalities were such that they kept their emotions inside or played with a lack of intensity simply had to change. We also stressed the importance of playing hard for the full 40 minutes. I think some of the guys thought they were playing hard all the time, but they weren't.

Coach said some things at the meeting, but he really didn't go off. He just pointed out areas where we needed improvement. Mostly, Rod and I did the talking. Like I said, there was no anger or dissension at all. It was one of those open discussions that most teams have a couple of times a year. Things needed to be said, and they were. That's the only way to it. It's when you keep feelings bottled in that you have dissension on a team. I don't think we were nearly as angry as we were confused. We'd just lost two games in a row, something we weren't used to. There's no doubt in my mind that the meeting brought us all closer together as a team. It's just too bad that it took back-to-back losses before we had our little chat.

Along about this time, I started hearing all the talk about how I was having such a bad year. People were whispering, "What's wrong with Travis?" or "Why isn't Travis scoring like he did last year?" I wasn't having a bad year at all. True, my shooting percentage was down from the previous year, but my assists were up and my overall team leadership had been steady. Unfortunately, many fans equate shooting with performance. If you're hitting the basket and scoring a ton of points, it's automatically assumed that you're playing well. Conversely, if you aren't hitting the basket and scoring big, you aren't playing well. That's simply not true, and anyone who really knows the game of basketball will tell you it's not true. I've had big scoring nights when I knew — and the coaches knew — that I hadn't played particularly well. It's never as simple as looking at the total points column and passing judgment based on what numbers are there.

Yes, my shooting was down, and I wouldn't be honest if I said it didn't concern me. But I never let it affect my game. In fact, because I wasn't hitting like I usually did, I concentrated on helping the team in other ways. Every good shooter goes through slumps. That's part of the game. All you can do is keep working hard, not let your confidence sag, and take the shot when it's there. You must never start to doubt yourself. When you do, that's when you get into real trouble. If it becomes a mental thing, the situation usually goes from bad to worse.

Part of my amazement (and amusement) with all the talk was the lack of insight from those who were doing most of the talking. It wasn't like I woke up one morning and couldn't shoot anymore. There were several obvious reasons why my shooting had fallen off. Like not having Jamal Mashburn as a teammate. Mash's presence opened things up for everyone else on the team. More than anyone, I probably benefited the most from Mash. Opponents concentrated so much on stopping him that they often forgot about me. I would roam around out on the perimeter until I got open, then Mash would hit me with a pass. Even when Mash didn't have the ball, he usually occupied one or two defenders. That translated into good shots for the rest of us. Losing Moon also played a role, no question about it. Not having him in the middle, and not having him to set screens on the perimeter, made it that much harder for me to consistently get good looks at the basket. And because of the year I had in 1992-93, I drew a lot of attention from opposing defenses. Coach Pitino once said that opponents were treating me like a lottery pick. Although most of the coaches didn't come right out and say it, they took the same approach as Nolan Richardson, who said, "Their head is Ford. If you cut the head off, the body doesn't function." I suppose I should be flattered by all that attention, but there were times when I would have preferred to be a complete unknown.

The majority of Big Blue fans are always on your side, but there are some who aren't happy unless they're being critical and judgmental. Those are the ones you just tune out because nothing short of perfection will please them. UK football coach Bill Curry has the perfect description for them — the fellowship of the miserable. That's exactly what they are.

If there ever was a time when the fellowship of the miserable was primed and ready to bring their negative message to the radio talk shows, it had to be when we were down by 31 in the second half at LSU. It was a perfect situation for anyone who thrives under a dark cloud. We'd lost two straight, and now here we were being absolutely destroyed by LSU, one of our most-hated rivals.

But we pulled the plug on their misery by mounting one of the greatest, most courageous comebacks in the history of college basketball. Given up for dead early in the second half, we fought back to score a miraculous 99-95 victory. It was an unforgettable moment for all of us, and probably the best win any of us had ever experienced. I know it was for me. There is no way we should have won that game. No way at all. Think about it... down by 31, second half, playing in LSU's arena against a team that is on fire that night. By all rights, we should have lost our third game in a row. We went into that game knowing that LSU wasn't a great team, but a dangerous one. So what happens? They come out and play the first half like they were the New York Knicks. Freshman guard Ronnie Henderson hit five three-pointers — three within a span of 61 seconds — to help the Tigers build a 48-32 lead at the half.

Clearly, our backs were up against the wall. We were in a hole in more ways than one. We didn't want to lose three in a row, and we didn't want to fall farther behind Florida in the SEC East Division standings. This was a game we had to have, but when we went into the dressing room at the half, our situation was pretty grim.

At the half, Coach Pitino told us to be patient and to make it a possession-by-possession game. He said if we wanted to overcome a deficit like that, we had to chip away at it a little at a time. If we rushed, he told us, or if we tried to make it up all at once, we would only dig ourselves into a deeper hole.

We came out wanting to do what he told us, but LSU, thanks to some unbelievable shooting by Henderson and Clarence Ceasar, couldn't be stopped. They seemed to score at will. If they put up a shot from anywhere on the court, it went in. Nothing we did slowed them down at all. They were just blowing us away.

With 15:34 left in the game, we were trailing 68-37. Down 31 points. Talk about being humbled. We were. I think by this time Coach Pitino had given up on us winning and was more concerned that a blow-out loss would do so much damage to our confidence that we'd never recover. And it probably would have, too. I'd hate to think what a 25 or 30-point loss at LSU would have done to us.

When we were down by 31, I got the guys together and said, "We're not leaving this building without a win, even if it means we have to stay all night." Later, when the reporters asked me if I really believed we could come back, naturally, I said yes. But the truth is, deep down, I'm not sure I did believe it. Probably, I hoped it more than I believed it.

But then something amazing began to happen. We hit a few threes, stopped them a couple of times on defense, and, suddenly, the momentum had shifted. I hadn't been paying any attention to the score, then I looked up and saw that we were down by only 19. A few minutes later, we had cut the lead to 13. So much was happening so fast that it was a blur to me. What I remember most are the nice inside moves by Gimel and the three-pointers that Jeff and Walter kept making. Especially Jeff's. He hit four that really ignited our comeback.

After we closed to within one at 96-95 with 19 seconds left, Walter put up a three from the left corner, right in front of our bench. The coaches were yelling for him to shoot and he did. Swish. Nothing but the bottom of the net. It was a gutty shot for a guy playing his first season of college basketball. No wonder we call him "Ice."

A few seconds later, we stopped LSU and got the ball back. They fouled me, and when I hit the two free throws, the game was ours. We had come back from the brink of defeat to score a win that had the whole world of college basketball buzzing for the next week.

What made it especially nice was that everybody made a contribution in that game. Chris Harrison came off the bench and hit two big threes, Walter had 23 points, Jeff had 14 and Gimel had 13. It was a total team win in the truest way.

Our dressing room was a madhouse after the game. I've never seen anything quite like it. We sat there and hugged and smiled and laughed for 30 or 40 minutes. No one wanted to take a shower and leave. This was a special moment, and we didn't want it to end. Coach Pitino said it was one of the greatest games he'd ever been a part of and that he'd never been more proud of a team. I think we were all proud at that moment. We could have cracked mentally, or given up, but we didn't. We hung in. We proved we had plenty of character. We showed real mental toughness.

Winning that game taught us all a great lesson. It showed what you can do, even under the most difficult circumstances, if you keep playing hard and don't give up. It also proved to us just how great Coach Pitino's system is. The way we shoot the three, press, and get up and down the floor, we're never out of a game.

One thing I've often wondered about — how many people actually stayed up and watched the entire game on television. Of course, everybody says they did, but I'll bet if the truth were known, there were a lot of people who didn't find out that we won until they read it in the morning paper. What a pleasant surprise that must have been for them.

CHAPTER SEVENTEEN

FOUL PLAY

Our next game was at Vanderbilt, and based on the outcome — we won 77-69 — it should have been cause for rejoicing. Beating Vandy in their gym isn't easy, yet we had gone down there and done it. That's something not many UK teams have been able to do in recent years. We did celebrate, too... for about two days. Then all hell broke loose, thanks to what would come to be known as "The Great Switcheroo Scandal."

The furor that arose came about because of two incidents during the Vandy game in which we put the wrong free throw shooter on the line. The first incident occurred when Jared was fouled and Gimel shot the free throws. At the time, Jared was zero-for-four at the line, so when he was fouled, as he and Gimel were walking up the court, Gimel said, "Do you want me to shoot the free throws for you?" Jared nodded and answered, "You might as well. I'm oh-for-four."

The incident that got me in all kinds of hot water was somewhat more complicated. Walter and Andre were fighting for the basketball when one of the officials called a foul on a

Vandy player. At that point, I didn't know which guy was fouled. Both of them were standing there, and the referee who made the call was running toward the scorer's table. Without hesitating, I told Walter to go to the line and shoot. It was pure instinct on my part. I wasn't thinking about right or wrong, only about winning the game. Since Walter is a much better free throw shooter than Andre, I knew it was in our best interest to have him at the line. I should have let the referee decide, but I really don't think he knew whether it was Walter or Andre who should be shooting.

At the time no one caught it, and it wasn't until after the game that someone did. Then, during a post-game interview, one of the local TV guys asked me about it. Like a dummy, and without thinking what I was saying, I admitted that we had indeed switched shooters. What's worse, I didn't just admit it, I laughed about doing it. That was an even bigger mistake than the original crime.

No one gave it any more thought until Monday night, which was when Coach first learned about it. Someone asked him about it on Big Blue Line, the radio call-in show. He responded by saying that it was the first he'd heard of it, but that he would check into it further.

He came straight from his show to Wildcat Lodge and called a team meeting. He was about as angry as I'd ever seen him. He was steaming. When we told him what we'd done, he said he was probably going to suspend us for the Tennessee game, and that he'd let us know the next morning after sleeping on it overnight.

At 7:30 on Tuesday morning, we had another team meeting. Coach was still very upset... he hadn't calmed down at all. During the meeting, he told the team that Gimel, Jared and I would not make the trip to Knoxville. When he said that, several of the players, particularly Rodrick and Jeff Brassow, argued for a less severe punishment, saying that the team needed the three of us at such a crucial time of the season. They were in favor of giving us extra study hall, or more running, or just about anything other than a suspension. Coach said no, a one-game suspension would be the best way to teach us a valuable lesson.

During the meeting, Coach asked me my version of what had happened. I told him that I did not know who got fouled and that I had acted on instinct when I directed Walter to the foul line. At first, Coach didn't believe me. He was suspicious, so he asked Jeff Brassow if he believed my story. Brass said he agreed with me 100 percent. Brass went on to say that I wouldn't do anything maliciously, that I didn't do it on purpose, that I was just trying to help us win, and that I shouldn't be suspended. Coach asked Brass why he believed me, and Brass said, "Because Travis is my roommate and my teammate." That answer didn't impress Coach at all. In fact, he got so angry that he kicked Brass out of the meeting.

At first, I was extremely bitter at Coach Pitino for what he had done. My initial feeling was that the whole thing was being blown way out of proportion. I just didn't think it was such a big deal. Another thing that troubled me at first was the fact that I was being suspended and Andre and Walter were not. I didn't see the fairness in that. By no means did I want them to be suspended — we needed them against Tennessee — but I couldn't shake the feeling that I was taking all of the blame for what had happened.

My feelings changed when I had a personal meeting with Coach Pitino later that morning. He made it clear to me that what I had done was wrong, and that no team of his would sacrifice integrity in favor of winning at all costs. One thing he said that really hit home with me was that the Vanderbilt players had worked as hard as we had to get into the NCAA Tournament, that they were on the bubble, and that a loss would hurt their post-season chances. He said it would be terribly unfair for them to get knocked out of the tourney because we beat them by doing something dishonest. When he put it that way, I realized that what I did was wrong, and that even though I didn't see it as cheating, I shouldn't have done it. I didn't like being suspended, and I didn't want to miss the Tennessee game, but I accepted the verdict Coach handed down.

Looking back on it, I know that I put Coach in a no-win situation by going on TV and bragging about what I had done. That was a dumb, immature act on my part. If I hadn't done that, perhaps Coach could have disciplined us in a different way. Maybe the whole thing would have quietly blown over. But once it became public knowledge, he had no other choice but to suspend us.

You have to respect Coach Pitino for what he did. He stood by his principles, even at the risk of losing a game that would all but kill our chances of winning the SEC East Division title. Not many coaches, in that exact situation, would have had the courage to do what he did.

Another immediate target of my anger and frustration was the media. I felt like they were fanning the flames with their endless stories and commentaries. I also felt that some of them had led me into saying things in the heat of the moment that I shouldn't have said. But blaming them was wrong. I made the mistake, so I was the only one to blame. I had to accept responsibility for my actions. One of the pitfalls of playing at the University of Kentucky is that everything you do, everything that happens to you, is magnified a thousand times. When a Kentucky Wildcat makes a mistake or does something wrong, everybody knows about it within minutes. Nothing ever happens to a UK player in a quiet way. Everywhere you looked, there was three mug shots, like we were criminals. We made national TV, the front page of the newspaper, the talk shows, everything. We became known as "The Switcheroo Gang." As you might expect, every time we went on the road during the rest of the season, that's all we heard about.

Consequently, when a UK player does foul up, the embarrassment is great. I was certainly embarrassed about what happened, but most of all, I felt that I had let a lot of people down. We had a crucial game with Tennessee coming up, and I wouldn't be playing. I was miserable until the Tennessee game was over.

Of course, being a UK player in times of trouble also has its upside. For the next couple of days, I must have gotten several dozen letters and phone calls from fans telling me they supported me, and for me to keep my head up. Many of them said they thought that what I did was a smart move and the right thing to do under the circumstances. Others said they stood behind me even though they thought that I had acted in an improper manner. Overall, the opinion of the fans regarding the incident was mixed. However, their support for me, Gimel and Jared never wavered.

About a month or so after the incident, I was watching an Orlando Magic game on TV and Scott Skiles did the same thing. After the game, one of the reporters asked him if he had seen what I did against Vandy. He said he had. He went on to say that he thought it was the best move he ever saw a college guard make, and that he loved watching me play because of that. That made me feel good because Scott Skiles is one of my favorite players. It was also interesting to hear a different perspective. Here's Scott Skiles, one of the best guards in the NBA, saying it's a smart move.

One final thing about that incident. Several opposing coaches, most notably Vandy's Jan Van Breda Kolff and Marquette's (now Tennessee's) Kevin O'Neill, said in public that they felt Coach Pitino knew about what happened and that we had probably been doing it all season. That's absolutely not true. Coach Pitino didn't know a thing about it. How could he? Both incidents, mine and the one involving Gimel and Jared, were strictly spur-of-the-moment. Nothing was planned in advance. It was a close game, and we were looking for an edge. We thought at the time that sending a better shooter to the free throw line was a smart move. We didn't see it as cheating. We were wrong to do it. It wasn't smart or clever, and it certainly wasn't the right thing to do. We made a mistake, we were punished for it, and we learned a lesson from it. Case closed.

Coach Van Breda Kolff was, and is, way out of line to say what he did. As a matter of fact, if Coach Van Breda Kolff thinks it was so obvious, why didn't he or the other Vandy coaches catch it at the time? Coach O'Neill is a good friend of mine and a man I have the utmost respect for, but I was disappointed when I read that he'd said some bad things about it. I don't see how coaches who aren't around our program, or who aren't familiar with us at all, can make such statements. It seems a little presumptuous to me.

Because the three of us weren't going to play against Tennessee, Coach Pitino didn't let us practice the day before the game. We hung around Wildcat Lodge, then after the team left for Knoxville, we went over to Memorial Coliseum to get in some shots and do a little conditioning. It was a weird feeling, knowing that the team had left to play a game and here we were back in Lexington.

We decided to watch the game together in the Lodge. We ordered a pizza, then went downstairs to watch on the big TV. Watching that game was one of the toughest things I've ever had to do. We wanted the guys to win so bad, yet there was nothing we could do to help. It was a frustrating feeling for all three of us. But we were great cheerleaders. And when a referee made a call we didn't agree with, we let him know about it. We were far more nervous watching the game than we would have been playing. Jared got so nervous that he wouldn't even come down to watch the second half. He stayed in his room by himself.

The eight guys who went down to Knoxville did the impossible — they beat Tennessee 77-73. Talk about a courageous effort. That was as gutty a performance as you'll ever see. Great UK teams have gone to Knoxville and lost, yet here you have these eight guys going down there and beating the Volunteers. Incredible.

Everyone played well in that game, but the player I was most proud of was Anthony Epps. He really stepped forward and ran the team like he was a senior rather than a freshman. He played with great poise, intelligence and confidence. At no time in that game did he crack under pressure. I wasn't surprised at all by the way Anthony played. I go against him everyday in practice, so I can tell you first-hand that he has improved on a daily basis. Anthony Epps will be an excellent point guard for the next three years. One of the positives to come out of a bad situation is that Anthony really came of age during the Tennessee game.

We were so excited that the guys had won in Knoxville that we drove out to the airport to meet them. We waited for close to an hour before they arrived, but when they did, it was celebration time. We congratulated them for a big win and told them that we were behind them 100 percent. I think more than anything, going to the airport that night made us feel like we were a part of the team again.

Things returned to normal the next day. It was back to business as usual for all of us. All was forgiven. Coach Pitino never held anything against us or said another word about what had happened. I think one of Coach's greatest qualities is that he never holds a grudge. He might get mad at you, and stay that way for a couple of hours, but then he forgets about it and puts it behind him. That's a quality not many people have.

In our next game, against Georgia in Rupp Arena, I had a very scary moment. It happened in the first half, and when it did, I thought that my college career was finished. I was headed down on a fast break, running as hard as I could, when all of a sudden, I felt this excruciating pain in the back of my leg. For a second or two, I thought I had been shot. I had never felt anything like it before. I couldn't move my leg... it was extremely tight. I thought that I had torn my ACL. Then I thought it was just a bad cramp and that it would go away in a minute or two. But it didn't go away, so they took me back into the dressing room to check it more closely. The doctor said I had pulled a hamstring, but to what extent wouldn't be known for sure until the next day. Naturally, I didn't think it was all that serious, even though the pain was still pretty intense. After a few minutes, when it did loosen up somewhat, I went out into the hallway to see if I could run or jump. I was going to try to play in the second half, but there was no way. Anytime I tried to run or put any pressure on it at all, it would just tighten up again.

We killed Georgia, 80-59. The game was tied at the half, but we outscored them 50-29 in the final 20 minutes to win easily. Tony had 22 in that game and Rodrick had 15. Chris Harrison came off the bench to hit three treys and score 12 points. It was his biggest scoring night of the season. I saw a lot of JoAnn Hauser over the next two days, getting treatment for my injury. JoAnn's the best. She does a great job of taking care of us. If it weren't for her, those of us who always seem to be getting hurt would never play. I wish I had a dollar for every hour that JoAnn has spent working with Jeff Brassow during the past few years. I'd be a wealthy man.

Fortunately, my injury wasn't too severe. Although I was still experiencing some discomfort, it wasn't going to keep me from playing against Florida. Not only was this an important SEC game, it was also my final home game as a Kentucky Wildcat. Seniors' Night is a special moment, one that never fails to bring about mixed emotions. On the one hand, you look forward to it, but on the other hand, you hope it never comes.

Running through the hoop, going to center court with Kim and my family, being joined by Jeff, Gimel, Moon, Henry Thomas and their families, hearing the Rupp Arena crowd cheering, listening to the singing of My Old Kentucky Home... it's a moment I'll never forget. Very emotional, very sentimental. While My Old Kentucky Home was being sung, I looked up at the championship banners, the Final Four banners and all the retired jerseys, and I couldn't help feeling extremely proud and honored to have been a part of UK's basketball history and tradition. Standing there, having all those people acknowledging us and thanking us for what we had done and what we had meant to them was a wonderful moment for all of the seniors.

One of the potential pitfalls of Seniors' Night is that the players become so emotionally spent that they have nothing left to give during the game. Staying focused is essential. That was especially true this time because our opponent was Florida, a club that had already defeated us earlier in the year. In addition to the revenge factor, there was also the matter of the league race. If we beat Florida at home and South Carolina on the road, then the East Division crown was ours.

The Florida game was every bit at tough as we expected it to be. We trailed early, and were down by 10 at the half, but we fought back and won a close one 80-77. I shot well in that game, hitting four of six three-point attempts for 12 points. Rod and Tony each had 18 points to lead us in scoring. One of the big keys to our victory was that we did a good job of checking the Florida guards. Dan Cross and Craig Brown only had 25 points between them. If you contain them, you can beat Florida.

With Florida behind us, we turned our attention to South Carolina, a team that gave us fits when we played them in Rupp Arena. We won that game, but not without a struggle. South Carolina may not have the best talent in the world, but they have one of the best coaches in the business in Eddie Fogler, who gets the most out of what he has.

We went to South Carolina knowing that a win would give us the division title and a No.1 seed in the SEC Tournament. Despite being really psyched up for the game, we came out and gave a less-than-inspired performance. We controlled the game until the final few minutes, then let them get back in it. We didn't put them away when we had the chance and that came back to haunt us. We lost 75-74 on a last-second shot.

It was a stunning defeat for all of us. And a major disappointment. So much was at stake, yet we didn't rise to the occasion. I thought we played hard, but when they made their comeback, we failed to answer. A big reason we didn't was because of me. I didn't show much leadership when I should have. I didn't make an extra effort to see that we ran the right offense or set up properly on defense. I should have done what I did at LSU, pull the guys together and tell them that we're not leaving here without a win. It was just a poor job on my part.

I refuse to make excuses, but the brutal schedule we had just gone through, and all the turmoil caused by the situation at Vandy, contributed greatly to our loss at South Carolina. We were so physically and emotionally fatigued that we didn't have anything left at the end of that game. We were so worn down that when we needed extra emotion and intensity, it wasn't there.

Coach Pitino was upset with us and he had every right to be. So much was on the line — division title, seedings, ranking —and as a coach, he was disappointed that we let it slip through our fingers.

When we landed back in Lexington, he kept the players on the plane for about 10 or 15 minutes. He said he understood that we had gone through a difficult stretch and that we were mentally whipped. But he also told us that if we wanted to be successful in the SEC tourney and the NCAA tourney, our whole attitude was going to have to change, that we had to get more confidence in ourselves, and that we were going to have to go out and play hard for the full 40 minutes. When he finished talking to us, he did something he'd never done before —he gave us two days off. Part of the reason he did that was to let us get some much-needed rest. Another reason is that he was so upset with the way we played at South Carolina that he didn't want to come to practice the next day with any negative feelings toward us.

We didn't care about reasons... all we knew was that time off was welcomed. With the post-season tournaments just a week away, we needed the rest. It had been a tough six weeks for all of us.

CHAPTER EIGHTEEN

SHOWTIME

The loss to South Carolina dropped us from a No. 1 seed to a No. 2 seed in the SEC tourney, but it had virtually no affect at all on our confidence. After the two days off, we were eager to get back on the court and begin preparations for our first-round game, which was against Mississippi State. The rest worked wonders for all of us. It allowed us to get our legs back, and it gave those of us who were nursing nagging injuries some additional time to recuperate.

If anything, losing to South Carolina made us angry. It also fueled our desire to prove the critics wrong. And at that point, our critics were many. Maybe critics isn't the right term to use... doubters is probably more accurate. After the loss at South Carolina, we took a real bashing from sports writers who questioned our heart and our pride. They said we weren't a very good basketball team. We finished the regular season with a 24-6 record against a murderous schedule, yet if you believed what was being written, we'd had a disasterous year. I don't think many writers or TV people gave us much of a chance to win the SEC tournament. We were being written off by just about everyone. Some people predicted that we would lose our tourney opener. Talk like that only drove us to work harder. We knew Mississippi State was a tough opponent, but we also knew there was no way we were going to let them beat us. Contrary to what the writers — and the Arkansas faithful were saying — we considered the SEC Tournament to be ours, and ours alone.

We beat Mississippi State without much trouble, winning 95-76, even though we didn't have Rodrick. He was suspended for breaking a team rule the night before we played. Jeff Brassow was inserted into the starting lineup, and he responded by scoring 19 points. He was terrific. Gimel and I each had 14 points, but the real star of the night was Tony. He bombed the Bulldogs into submission with 29 points.

That win brought us face to face with Arkansas in the semifinal round. Proud, cocky Arkansas, a team that had beaten us twice in Rupp Arena in the past three years. This was the showdown everyone was waiting for.

The only thing we heard all week was that no one could beat Arkansas in The Pyramid. Memphis is so close to Arkansas that Razorback fans dubbed The Pyramid "Barnhill East." To them, playing there was like playing a home game.

We didn't care what their fans thought, just like we paid no attention to those people who claimed that we had little or no chance to win. We knew we could beat Arkansas, if we played the full 40 minutes with the same intensity and enthusiasm that we had during the first half of our regular season game with them. We stayed cool and didn't get too excited if we got way ahead or fell behind. We handled their pressure, rebounded strong, and didn't give them easy layups. We played with confidence, with a genuine belief that we could win. The game was a war from the opening tip-off, with both teams going eyeball to eyeball for the full 94-feet. This time, however, when it came to crunch time, it was Arkansas who blinked.

We spoiled the big Hog party by carving out a 90-78

win, and we did it by giving one of our best, most consistent efforts all season. And everyone who played chipped in. Tony had 16 points, Rod 14, Jeff and Jared 12 each. I also played well, scoring 15 points with eight assists.

We had followed the same script as last year, beating them in the SEC tourney after they had beaten us during the regular campaign. I hate to lose to anyone, anytime, but if I have to lose, I'd rather have it happen during the regular season than during the post-season tournaments. A loss in the SEC tourney can shake a team's confidence heading into the NCAA tourney, and a loss in the NCAA ends your season.

We were all very excited about making it to the finals of the SEC Tournament again and even more excited that we were going to get a rematch against Florida. They beat us out for the SEC East Division title, which we felt we should have won. Plus, there were a lot of folks who said that Florida had a better team than us. This game meant a lot to us because even though they won the regular season league division title, we were determined to show everyone that when it came to the tournament, we were still the team to beat.

Florida played us tough, like we knew they would, but when the final buzzer sounded, the tournament championship belonged to us for the third straight year. We won 73-60.

One of the things I'm most proud of is that we never lost an SEC Tournament game in the three years that I've played here. In those three years, we played nine games and won them all. We have that kind of remarkable success because Coach Pitino's teams take a different approach during tournament time than most teams take. Most of them play not to lose the game; we play to win the game. They tend to get more conservative once the tournaments begin, while we try to play less conservatively. One of our tournament goals is to score more points than we did during the regular season. Another big reason for our success is our style of play. We get up and down the court, shoot the threes, and press. However, the biggest reason of all is the way we prepare. Our coaching staff has the ability to get us prepared for an opponent in just one night. Because of that, we always go into a game knowing exactly what the other team is going to do. Nothing is left to chance, and that gives us a huge edge. No team in the country is better prepared than we are.

Winning the tournament again this year didn't surprise me at all. I felt all along that if we played up to our potential, we would win it. I was surprised, however, when I was named the tourney MVP again. That came totally out of the blue. I'm always surprised when anything like that happens, but never more so than this year. I didn't have the big scoring nights that you usually see from an MVP. But it's like Coach Pitino told me after the game, the people who voted for me did so because they thought that I was a leader out on the court and that I was very valuable to my team. It was rewarding to me, but it's something you can't possibly win unless you have great teammates. We had several other guys who had a great tournament, and I really thought that any one of three or four guys on our team could have won it.

Without question, one of the most satisfying moments came when Jeff Brassow was named to the all-tournament team. After all the things he's been through, all the pain and discomfort he's had to endure, to watch him step into the starting lineup and have the kind of tournament he had was something special. He went out and played just like he always does, making things happen, giving up his body for a rebound or a loose ball, making the extra pass, and knocking down the threes when he's open. Jeff really came up big for us in Memphis, and no one was happier for him than I was.

After we won the tournament, we hurried up to the press room to watch the NCAA pairings show on TV. Before the show began, Coach Pitino got a call on his mobile phone from someone who told him that we were a No. 3 seed in the Southeast Regional. When Coach told us, we thought he was kidding. We thought for sure that we had a two seed wrapped up. We'd beaten the No. 1 team in the country, we'd won the

SEC tourney, and going into the NCAA Tournament, we were ranked in the AP's Top 10. Plus, a lot of highly ranked teams had lost during that weekend. Naturally, we were disappointed when we learned that we weren't a two seed. In our hearts, we truly believed we had earned it. The one positive was that we would be playing in the Southeast Regional, meaning more of our fans would be able to watch us play.

We didn't know much about our opponent, Tennessee State, other than that they had Carlos Rogers, a potential first-round NBA draft pick. Because I had played with Carlos in the World University Games the previous summer, Coach Pitino really picked my brain about him. So did my teammates. They wanted to know what to expect from Carlos. From that stand- point, I was able to help the coaches and my teammates prepare for the game. What I told them was that I don't think we played against a player all season who was as capable of dominating a game like Carlos could. He was the OVC Player of the Year two years in a row, and he'd had several 40-point scoring nights in the past, so our first order of business was to shut him down. Carlos is the kind of player who could almost win a game singlehandedly.

During the week leading up to the game, the Tennessee State players said a lot of things in the paper, how they would beat us, how much better they were than us, how they should be the favorites and we should be the underdogs. They said if we played them at their place, they would beat us by 20 points. Even their coach was saying some things like that. Our coaches cut those stories out of the paper, highlighted what the Tennessee State players said, and put them in our lockers. When we read all that junk, it gave us an extra incentive to beat their brains in.

Without question, the most fired-up player on our team was Andre. Most people generally assumed that the post play between Andre and Rogers would be a mismatch, with Rogers getting the big edge in every department. Andre wasn't going to settle for second best, not after hearing and reading about how he was going to get creamed by Rogers. Andre took this game as a personal challenge, and was determined to go out and prove the so-called "experts"wrong. And he did just that, completely outplaying Rogers in every area.

Andre was like a man possessed, rebounding, defending, dunking, and hitting that little jump-hook that he developed during the last half of the season. We won the game 83-70, and Andre was a big reason why. He scored 22 points, tying Rod for team-high honors. Rod also played very well, using his great athleticism and his ability to slash to the bucket to great advantange. The Tennessee State defenders had a hard time keeping up with Rod, who has a lightning-quick first step. As a result, Rod went to the foul line 19 times, hitting 13. Tony had 13 points and I had 10. However, I wasn't pleased with my performance. I committed six turnovers, which is far too many.

We knew the Marquette game would be a real test for us because they had one of the best defenses in the country. And there was also the matter of contrasting styles. They play a very deliberate style, which is, of course, the exact opposite of ours. They're a pattern team that likes to run a patient offense. When you throw in two seven-footers in the middle and one of the best power forwards around, you're facing one of the strongest inside games in all of college basketball. Even with all of that to deal with, we were certain that we could contain them.

So much of our success depended on how well we hit the basket. Everything else, most especially our defense, fed off of our shooting. The higher our shooting percentage, the more times we could get into our full-court press. The more we pressed, the more easy layups we got. Contrary to what most people believe, Coach Pitino stresses the importance of defense much more he stresses the importance of offense. The reason for that is simple: When it comes to tournament time, defense usually wins games.

The absolute worst nightmare of any team — or player — is to come out in the NCAA Tournament and have a miserable shooting night. That's our greatest fear. And that's exactly what happened against Marquette. We went through long periods where we couldn't throw one in the ocean. Marquette's defense had something to do with that, of course, but not everything. If you go back and watch the tape of that game, you'll see that we had plenty of wide-open shots. We were getting good looks at the baskets, but we just couldn't consistently get the shots to go down.

To be successful from the perimeter, you have to have a good inside game. They complement each other. An efficient outside game opens up the middle for the big guys. And vice versa. Against Marquette, our big guys weren't able to get much done. Because of that, it put added pressure on the perimeter players to pick up the slack. When a player feels that kind of pressure, he tends to either rush his shots or possibly take some that he shouldn't have taken. That's what happened against Marquette, and I think the proof is in the numbers. We made just 27 of 76 shots overall for 31.6 percent. From behind the three-point line, we hit just 10 of 38. With those kinds of numbers, it's little wonder that Marquette didn't beat us by more than 12 points (75-63).

I'm not pointing fingers or laying the blame on our inside people. No way I would ever do that. Goodness knows, there have been dozens of times during the season when they picked up the perimeters guys. It just shows you how crazy and unpredictable sports can be. And how quickly it can humble you. One night, you're on top of the world; the next night, you're so low you just want to go off and disappear for good. Take Rod, for instance. He gets 22 points against Tennessee State, then gets shut out against Marquette. How tough is that? And the thing is, he played just as hard against Marquette as he did against Tennessee State. One night belonged to him, the next night didn't. That's one of the cruelties of sports. What makes it even tougher is that the fans always seem to remember what you did in your last game and not necessarily remember what you've done overall. Of course, that's terribly unfair to Rod, or to anyone else who experiences something like that.

Despite our poor shooting, we still could have beaten Marquette. We had our chances, especially late in the second half when we cut their 15-point halftime lead down to 56-54. We trailed 39-24 at the half, then thanks to Tony's 12 quick points and a three by Jeff Brassow, we went on a 15-3 run that brought us to within 42-39. After falling behind 56-47 with a little over eight minutes remaining, Tony and I each hit a three and Jared made one of two free throws to make it 56-54. Things were looking good for us at that point... the momentum was ours. More important, it looked like we were finally starting to hit the basket. But that wasn't the case. In fact, we went stone cold, and that killed us. In the final three or four minutes, with the game on the line, Marquette executed better than us in all phases of the game. As Coach Pitino would later say, they were just better than us that day.

After the game, Coach told us how much he enjoyed all the seniors and how we'd had a lot of wonderful moments during our years at Kentucky. He said it had been his pleasure to coach us. Mostly, though, he focused more on the guys who were coming back, pointing out to them that they needed to work harder in the off-season and rededicate themselves if they wanted to come back and have a better team next season.

Since the season ended, a lot of people have asked me why this team didn't do better than it did. I've often asked myself the same question. Even though we finished with a 27-7 record, which is outstanding, I can't shake the feeling that we should have done better than that.

Looking at it now, I'd have to say that we just never did develop a great team chemistry. I don't know why, but we didn't. We had such great talent, but I don't think we ever used it in the right way. We had Rodrick, a tremendous one-on-one player, and Tony, a natural scorer, but our inside game, even though we had some good players who had good moments,was very inconsistent at times. I think that's what it all boils down to: lack of good team chemistry and an inside game that wasn't as potent as it would have been if Rodney Dent hadn't gone down with his injury.

But you know what? I don't think any of us should have to apologize or make excuses after finishing with a 27-7 record. When you consider the loss of Moon, our vicious schedule, and the fact that we were basically a very young team, I'd say we did just fine. Every player on this year's team has a right to be proud of what we accomplished. I know I am.

CHAPTER NINETEEN

SIZING IT UP

Not long ago, while attending the Boys' State Tournament in Louisville, a group of young kids came up to me and asked for my autograph. After I'd finished signing 15 or 20 of them, someone asked me a great question: Did I think I'd have withdrawal symptoms when the fans stopped making such a big fuss over me? That's something I've often wondered about. How will I feel when I'm no longer the center of attention? When I'm just another face in the crowd? And it's going to happen, too. You can count on that. The door never stops revolving... that's just the nature of things. Today's hero is tomorrow's trivia. I don't have any problem with that at all. I've had my time in the spotlight; now it's time for someone else to take my place. I only hope the ones who come along in the future are treated as well as I was and have as much fun as I did. If they do, they'll be lucky. The autograph thing, the cheer of the crowds, being in the glare of the spotlight... I don't think I'll miss those things all that much. Maybe I'm mistaken, but I don't think so. What I will miss, though, are my team mates. I will truly miss them. At Kentucky, when you play for Coach Pitino, the team becomes like a family. You go through so much together, both good and bad, that you develop a special kind of relationship. It's a unique and wonderful thing, and I'm going to miss not being a part of it anymore. I can do without playing in the games, but when it comes to not living in Wildcat Lodge and not being part of a team, that's different. The camaraderie is what I'll miss the most. That won't be so easy to get over.

Another person I know I'm going to miss is Bill Keightley. "Mr. Wildcat" is like a second father to all of us. He takes care of us 100 percent. Win or lose, he's always there for us. Perhaps more than anyone else, he's what Kentucky basketball is all about. I'll miss Mr. Keightley, but he's a guy I can always come back to. No matter when you played, if you're a Kentucky Wildcat, he'll always be in your corner.

I'll probably experience some strange feelings when next season rolls around and I'm not out there with the guys. Emptiness, sadness, pride, excitement, anticipation... I'm sure I'll feel all that and a lot more. Not being a Kentucky Wildcat will take some getting used to. Don't worry, next year's team will get along fine without Travis Ford. In fact, next year's club could be very, very good. When I think of next year, I think of Mark Pope. I can promise all Wildcat fans that he's going to be a major addition. Mark will be a real impact player. He'll fill many of the holes that were problem areas for us this past season. But next year's team still has some areas that need to be addressed if it hopes to reach its full potential. A lot of improvement has to be made over the summer. There is enough talent and ability to be the top team in the country, but for that to happen, virtually every player is going to have to have a big summer. Several players have to gain weight, some need to work on their shooting, and others need to work on their all-around game. If they do those things — and I believe they will — the sky is the limit. As far as replacing me at point guard, that won't be a problem. Anthony Epps, who improved greatly as the season progressed, and Allen Edwards, who is coming in as a freshman, are more than capable of doing an excellent job. Unless something totally unexpected happens, I think Kentucky will have a great, great season in 1994-95. Where will I be? Good question. And, as of this moment, one that I can't answer. About all I can tell you for certain is that Kim and I are getting married at her home in Bowling Green on Aug. 27. Beyond that, my future is uncertain.

My goal, of course, is to make it in the NBA. Whether that happens or not, no one can say. It'll be the toughest challenge I've ever faced, but playing at the pro level has been a dream of mine since I first picked up a basketball, so I'm going to give it a shot. I've got some opportunities to try out at NBA camps in Phoenix and Portsmouth, Ohio. I'll go there, do the best that I can, and see what happens. At least, I'll have a shot at it. But I'm realistic... someone my size would have to get certain breaks in order to make it. I hope I can play at the next level, but if I can't, I think I'm smart enough to do something else. It's the general assumption of most people that I'll eventually end up in the coaching ranks. I'd say that's very likely to happen. I can never see myself ever getting out of basketball. It has always been a big part of my life and, hopefully, it always will be. I really think I've learned enough from Coach Pitino that I could someday be a coach and do a good job at it.

Given the choice, I'd definitely prefer to coach at the college level, mainly because I would love to go out on the road. I love watching high school games, high school players, traveling... all the essential things it take to be a successful recruiter. Because I've been involved in so much at the college level, that's where I think I could do the best job. I wouldn't rule out coaching at the high school level, but I don't think it would be my first choice.

I don't know if Kim wants me to get into coaching because of the hours coaches have to put in, so she may have something to say about what happens. But I know she'll support me in whatever I choose to do. She's always been behind me all the way. She understands that success at anything never comes without a price. We both know that if I do get into coaching, it won't be easy on either of us. I don't know for sure, but my guess is that if she had her preference, she'd rather I do something other than coaching. I'm not a person who cares much for looking back. Reading about or thinking about what has already happened doesn't hold much interest for me. That's why doing a book like this is difficult. My feeling is that the past is over, so let's move forward and focus on the future rather than the past.

I am, however, going to go say one final thing about the past. If I don't, then my story won't be complete. I have to tell you — or at least try to tell you — what it's meant to me to be a Kentucky Wildcat. I say try to because I'm not sure I can even begin to express my feelings. Simply stated, playing basketball at the University of Kentucky has meant everything to me. Everything. I grew up in this state, so I know what UK basketball means to the fans. I know, because I was a fan long before I was a player. I cheered for Kyle Macy, Jay Shidler, Sam Bowie, Kenny Walker, Rex... all of the Wildcats. I stayed up to watch the delayed telecasts. I kept up with UK while I was at Missouri. UK was my team, and more than anything else, I dreamed of someday wearing a Wildcat uniform. Having seen that dream come true, having had the opportunity to play at UK and to follow all those great Wildcats who came before me, is something I'll always cherish. It was a remarkable and wonderful experience I'll remember always.